Contents

The material for years 3, 4 and 5 of SMP 1	
Introduction to *Book Y3*	5
Notes and answers for *Book Y3*	9
1 Stretching and enlargement	9
2 Linear relationships	10
If all you have is . . . (pages 23–4)	17
3 Vectors	18
Algebra review (1)	23
4 Percentage (1)	23
5 Mappings	25
6 Investigations (1)	31
Review 1	33
7 TV programmes survey	36
If all you have is . . . (page 67)	37
8 Direct and inverse proportionality	38
9 Representing information	39
Algebra review (2)	42
10 Looking at data	42
If all you have is . . . (page 91)	43
11 Percentage (2)	44
12 Investigations (2)	47
Algebra review (3)	48
13 Right-angled triangles	48
Review 2	51
14 Volume	52
15 Problems in planning	53
16 Linear equations	57
17 Distributions	58
Review 3	62

The School Mathematics Project was founded in 1961 with the purpose of improving the teaching of mathematics in schools by the provision of new course materials. SMP authors are experienced teachers and each new venture is tested by schools in a draft version before publication.

Work on SMP 11–16 started in 1977 and the pilot version of the course has been used by some 50 schools, most of them comprehensive but including some selective schools, since 1980. The published version of the course started appearing in 1983.

Since its inception the SMP has always offered an 'after sales service' for teachers using its materials. If you have any comments on SMP 11–16 or would like advice on its use please write to
SMP Office
University of Southampton
Southampton
SO9 5NH

The following people have contributed to the planning and writing of the Y, B and R series of books.

Graham Ambridge	Phil Goodwin	Brian Hughes
Chris Belsom	Eric Gower	Spencer Instone
Neil Bibby	Harry Gurevitch	Sylvia Johnson
Michael Darby	Graham Hall	John Ling
Charles Dickinson	Joyce Harris	Alan Mace
David Fenton	Ray Harris	Paul Scruton
Tony Gardiner	Stephen Horner	Martyn Truman
		Richard Walker

Others too numerous to be mentioned individually have provided valuable advice and help. Among these are the mathematics staff and pupils of the pilot schools whose detailed comments on the draft version were essential in revising the course for publication.

The SMP 11–16 team is led by John Ling.

With unfailing care the bulk of the manuscripts were typed for the press by Muriel Hudson. The authors wish to give particular thanks to Sue Glover for her work in preparing the materials for publication.

The material for years 3, 4 and 5 of SMP 11–16

The yellow, blue, red and green series together make up the second part of the SMP 11–16 course, for pupils in the third to fifth years of secondary school (ages 13+ to 16+).

(The booklet scheme which forms the first part of the course is fully described in the *Teacher's guides* for levels 1, 2, 3 and 4, and the *Practical guide*.)

The overall structure of the material for years 3 to 5 is set out in the diagram opposite.

The Y series is for the most able group of pupils (roughly speaking, the top 20% to 25% or so, although the proportion is likely to vary from school to school). The B and R series are for the 'middle' group (the next 35% to 40% or so) and the G series for lower ability pupils (apart from those with special learning difficulties).

The B series branches after *Book B2* to allow the more able of the pupils in the middle group to move ahead on to more demanding work in the R series. The mathematical content of the R series has much in common with that of *Books Y1, Y2* and *Y3*, but presentation and pace are often different.

The two YE books are 'extension' books written to stretch the most able pupils. *Books YT* and *BT* are transition books written for pupils who have not previously followed the booklet scheme in years 1 and 2.

Classroom organisation and teaching style

It is assumed that pupils will be grouped in sets according to ability in the third, fourth and fifth years.

Although there is rather more exposition and explanation in the books than is found in many other textbooks, the books are not intended to be 'self-instructional'. (This is particularly true of the chapters on algebra.) Many important points arise in the course of doing the problems in the books, and these points will need to be brought out by the teacher in discussion with the class or with smaller groups, as appropriate. Teachers may find it possible from time to time to give particular chapters or sections of chapters to the class to work through on

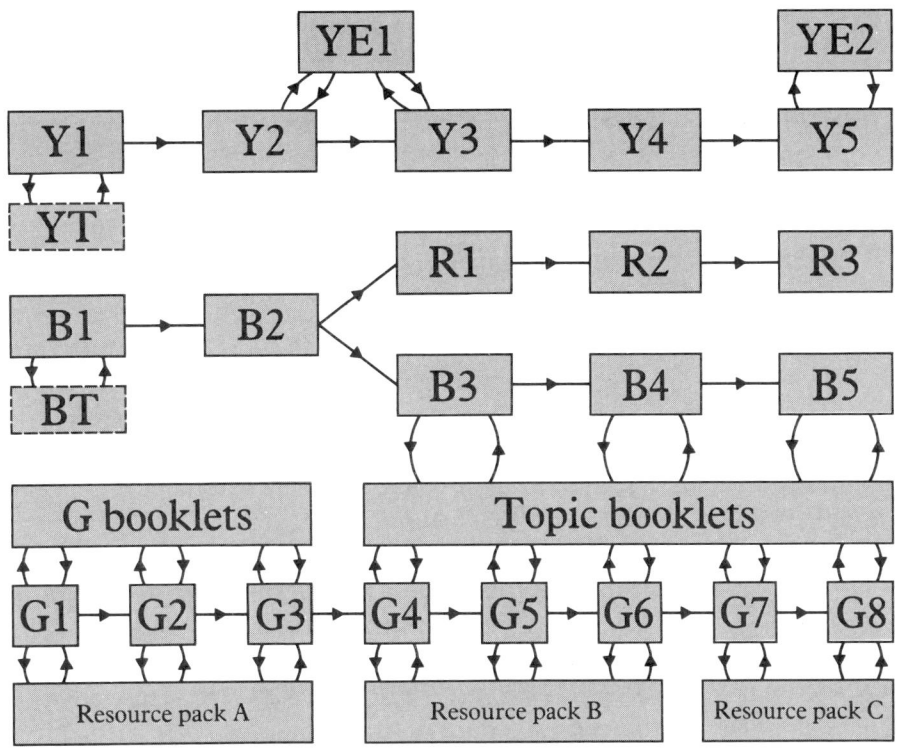

their own, which is no bad thing since the ability to pick up information from the printed page and to follow written explanations is an important one. Where this is done it will be necessary for the teacher carefully to 'go over' what has been done. Amongst pupils working from the Y series there may be some very able ones who are quite capable of forging ahead with understanding, working from the book alone, and who should not be 'kept back'. However it is not intended that working individually through the book should be the normal method of teaching for any class, whichever series it is using. (Exceptions to this are *Books YE1* and *YE2*, and the transition books *BT* and *YT*, which are written specifically for individual use.)

There are no 'chapter summaries'. The writers feel it is more valuable for classes to make their own summary notes. The ideal ultimately is for each pupil to make his or her own notes, but initially it may be better for the teacher to lead, after each chapter, a discussion of the main ideas before any notes are made.

Introduction to Book Y3

Mental and written arithmetic and the use of calculators

It is assumed throughout that unless there is an instruction to the contrary calculators will be used for all but the simplest calculations which can be done mentally.

We strongly recommend that teachers encourage mental calculation, and from time to time give short sets of questions to be answered mentally. We also suggest having occasional practice sessions on written arithmetic, but that the scope of these should not extend beyond addition, subtraction, multiplication by 2, 3, . . . , 9 and division by 2, 3, . . . , 9 of whole numbers and money.

Starred questions

Occasional questions are starred to indicate that they are of greater difficulty, and can be left out by slower pupils using the book.

Equipment needed for *Book Y3*

Certain standard items of equipment are needed frequently and no special attention is drawn to them in the books. These include rulers, angle measurers (recommended rather than protractors for angle measurement; see below), compasses, scissors and 2 mm graph paper.

In other cases, equipment needed (such as tracing paper) is referred to in the book. Worksheets are needed occasionally. Masters for these are available separately (see below). Four worksheets are needed for *Book Y3*, numbered Y3–1 to Y3–4.

Pupils working from the Y series are assumed to have the use of a scientific calculator from *Book Y2* onwards.

Ordering equipment

The following items required for *Book Y3* are published by Cambridge University Press. You should order them through your usual school book supplier.

Worksheet masters for *Books B3, R1* and *Y3*   ISBN 0 521 32417 3
Angle measurers (pack of 5)   ISBN 0 521 25435 3

When ordering, remember to state the ISBN, the series title (SMP 11–16), the name of the item, the publisher and the number of **packs** you want. (So, for example, if you want 35 angle measurers, write your order as '7 packs of 5'.)

Notes and answers for Book Y3

1 Stretching and enlargement

This chapter introduces one-way and two-way stretches and their effects on area. Enlargement is treated as a particular case of a two-way stretch in which the stretch factor is the same in both directions.

A One-way stretch

A1 Probably by measuring the distance of X from the left-hand edge and multiplying by the stretch factor

A2 Stretch factor 2·5

A3 Pupil's own drawing and stretch factor

A4 Stretch factor 3·6 (to 1 d.p.)

A5 (a)

Before stretching	After stretching
A 4 cm²	A′ 12 cm²
B 1 cm²	B′ 3 cm²
C 2 cm²	C′ 6 cm²
Total 7 cm²	Total 21 cm²

(b) Multiply by 3

A6 (a)

Before stretching	After stretching
A 6 cm²	A′ 12 cm²
B 3 cm²	B′ 6 cm²
C 3 cm²	C′ 6 cm²
Total 12 cm²	Total 24 cm²

(b) Multiply by 2

A7 (a) 8 cm² (b) 12 cm²
(c) Multiply by 1·5, the stretch factor

A8 (a) 5 cm² (b) 20 cm² (c) 50 cm²

B Stretching a circle

B1 See diagram.

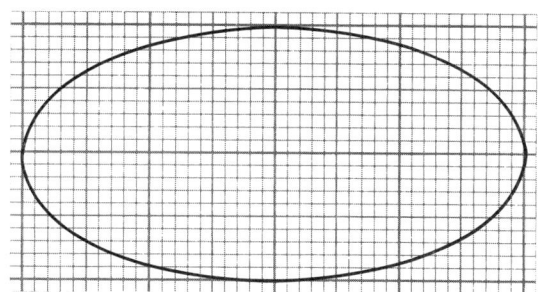

B2 (a) 12·57 cm² (to 2 d.p.)
(b) 25·13 cm² (to 2 d.p.)

B3 (a) 1·5 (b) 6·16 cm² (to 2 d.p.)
(c) 9·24 cm² (to 2 d.p.)

B4 (a) Stretch factor 2·49 (b) 11·95 cm²
(c) 29·71 cm² (all to 2 d.p.)

B5 9·42 cm² (to 2 d.p.)

C Two-way stretches

C1 (a)

Before	After
A 1 cm²	A′ 6 cm²
B ½ cm²	B′ 3 cm²
C 2 cm²	C′ 12 cm²
D 1 cm²	D′ 6 cm²

(b) Multiply by 6

C2 (a) 7 cm² (b) 140 cm²

C3 63 cm²

C4 (a) 3·14 cm² (b) 11·8 cm² (both to 3 s.f.)

9

C5 (a) Across, 3; up, 2
 (b) 18.8cm^2 (to 3 s.f.)

D Enlargement and reduction

D1 (a) Length, 20 cm; height, 8 cm
 (b) Area before, 10cm^2; area after, 160cm^2
 (c) The area is multipied by 16.

D2 (a) Length, 25 cm; height, 10 cm
 (b) Area before, 10cm^2; area after, 250cm^2
 (c) The area is multiplied by 25.

D3 (a) 36 (b) 100 (c) 4 (d) 64 (e) 49

D4 200cm^2

D5 (a) 25 (b) 81 (c) 6.25 (d) 12.25
 (e) 2.999 824

D6 This is a useful question for discussing the cumulative effects of small differences in measuring.
 (a) Length of P, 3.8 cm; length of Q, 6.2 cm; scale factor 1.6 (to 1 d.p.)
  (or 1.7 if using 3.7 cm for P)
 (b) Area factor 2.7 (to 1 d.p.)
  (or 2.8 if using 3.7 cm for P)
 (c) Area of Q, 10.1cm^2 (to 1 d.p.)
  (or 10.7cm^2 if using 3.7 cm for P)

*__D7__ $\sqrt{2} = 1.414$ (to 3 d.p.)

D8 (a) 5cm^2 (b) 3.2cm^2

D9 (a) $\frac{1}{4}$ (b) $\frac{1}{9}$ (c) 0.16
 (d) 0.09 (e) 0.01

D10 6.624cm^2

D11 This is another useful question for discussion about appropriate accuracy.
 (a) Length of A, 3.9 cm; length of B, 1.6 cm; scale factor 0.4
 (b) Area of B, 0.91cm^2 (to 2 d.p.)
  (using unrounded scale factor of 0.41025...; 0.86cm^2 using scale factor of 0.4)

D12 (a), (b) It is unlikely that many pupils will opt for A at first sight and their estimated fractions are therefore usually a long way out.
 (c) Width of shield: 4.0 cm
  Widths of outlines: A 2.8 cm, B 2.6 cm, C 2.4 cm
  Scale factors: A 0.7, B 0.65, C 0.6
 (d) Area factors: A 0.49, B 0.42 (to 2 d.p.), C 0.36

*__D13__ $\sqrt{\frac{1}{10}} = 0.316$ (to 3 d.p.)

*__D14__ (a) 800cm^2 (b) 450cm^2
 (c) 1512.5cm^2 (d) 1800cm^2

---

2 Linear relationships

The idea of gradient is extended to include the distinction between positive and negative gradients, and the chapter leads on to the gradient–intercept form of the equation of a straight line.

A Gradients of lines

A1 (a) $\frac{1}{2}$ (b) 3 (c) $\frac{3}{2}$ (d) 3
 (e) $\frac{1}{4}$ (f) $\frac{3}{4}$ (g) 1 (h) 6

A2 (b) and (d) have the same gradient so they are parallel.

A3 $\frac{3}{5}$

A4 (a) $\frac{5}{3}$ (b) $\frac{1}{2}$ (c) $\frac{1}{2}$ (d) $\frac{8}{5}$ (e) $\frac{2}{5}$
 (f) 3

B Positive and negative gradients

B1 (a) $^-1$ (b) $^-2$ (c) $\frac{2}{3}$
 (d) $^-\frac{2}{3}$ (e) $^-\frac{1}{9}$ (f) $\frac{1}{3}$

B2 (a) $-\frac{1}{2}$ (b) -3 (c) $\frac{5}{2}$
(d) -1 (e) $-\frac{1}{7}$

B3 (a) $\frac{1}{2}$ (b) -1 (c) $\frac{7}{3}$
(d) $-\frac{2}{7}$ (e) $\frac{6}{7}$ (f) $-\frac{3}{2}$

B4 (a) (i) 3 (ii) $-\frac{1}{3}$ (iii) $-\frac{3}{2}$
(iv) $\frac{2}{3}$ (v) $\frac{1}{4}$ (vi) -4
(b) Take the reciprocal and change the sign (or equivalent).
(c) $\frac{4}{3}$

B5 (a) b and f, c and g
(b) a and b, a and f, c and e, d and h, e and g

B6 The calculation involves dividing by zero and therefore the gradient is undefined.

C Gradient and intercept

C1 (a) $C = 3l$
(b), (d)

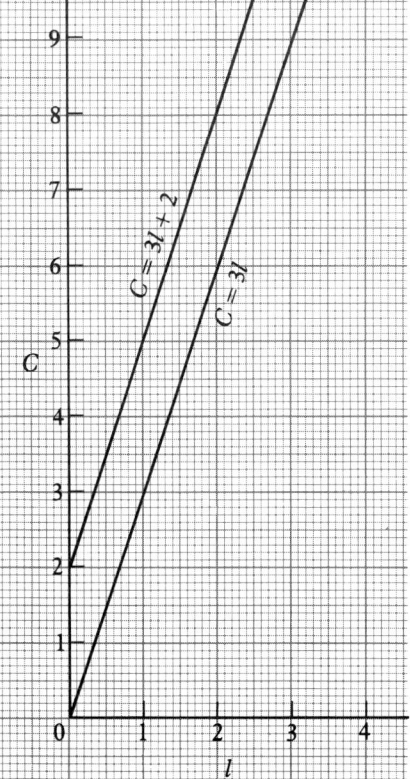

(c) $C = 3l + 2$
(e) 3 (f) 3 (g) 2

C2 (a) £5 (assuming the same units as before)
(b) £4 (c) 5 (d) 4

C3 (a)
x	0	2	4	6	8	10
y	0	1	2	3	4	5

(b), (d)

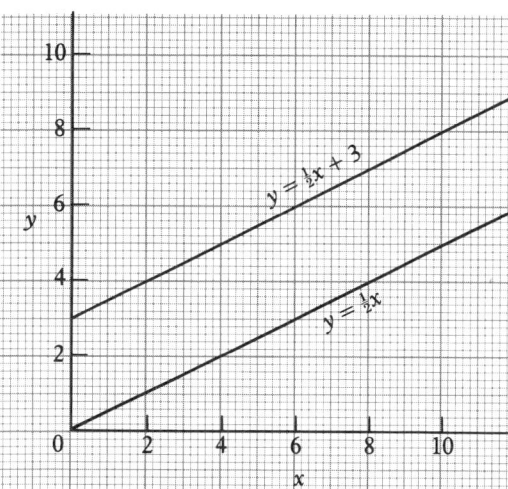

(c)
x	0	2	4	6	8	10
y	3	4	5	6	7	8

(e) $\frac{1}{2}$ (f) 3

C4 (a)
x	0	1	2	3	4	5
y	-3	-1	1	3	5	7

(b)

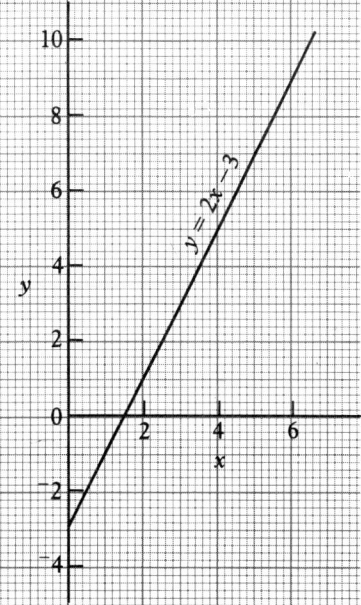

(c) 2 (d) $^-3$

C5 (a) (i) 3 (ii) 4 (b) (i) 7 (ii) 2
(c) (i) 7 (ii) $^-2$ (d) (i) $\frac{1}{3}$ (ii) $^-4$
(e) (i) 1 (ii) 3 (f) (i) 6 (ii) $^-6$
(g) (i) 4 (ii) 5 (h) (i) 2 (ii) $^-4$

C6 (a) $y = 1\cdot5x + 4$ (b) $y = 1\cdot5x + 3$
(c) $y = 1\cdot5x + 2$ (d) $y = 1\cdot5x + 1$
(e) $y = 1\cdot5x - 1$ (f) $y = 1\cdot5x - 2$

C7 (a) $\frac{1}{3}$ (b) $y = \frac{1}{3}x$ (c) $y = \frac{1}{3}x + 2$

C8 (a) 2 (b) 1 (c) $y = 2x + 1$
(d) $y = \frac{1}{3}x + 4$ (e) $y = \frac{1}{5}x + 2$

D2 (a) (i) $^-5$ (ii) 1 (b) (i) $^-5$ (ii) $^-2$
(c) (i) $0\cdot1$ (ii) $^-3\cdot8$ (d) (i) $^-4$ (ii) 7

D3 (a) $y = ^-\frac{1}{2}x + 4$ (b) $y = ^-\frac{1}{2}x + 3$
(c) $y = ^-\frac{1}{2}x + 2$ (d) $y = ^-\frac{1}{2}x + 1$
(e) $y = ^-\frac{1}{2}x - 1$ (f) $y = ^-\frac{1}{2}x - 2$
(g) $y = ^-\frac{1}{2}x - 3$

D4 (a) $^-\frac{1}{3}$ (b) $^-\frac{1}{3}$ (c) $y = ^-\frac{1}{3}x + 4$

D5 (a) (i) $^-3$ (ii) 5 (iii) $y = ^-3x + 5$
(b) $y = \frac{1}{3}x + 1$ (c) $y = ^-\frac{1}{3}x + 1$
(d) $y = ^-x - 1$ (e) $y = \frac{1}{4}x - 4$

D Lines with negative gradients

D1 (a)

x	0	2	4	6	8	10
y	0	$^-1$	$^-2$	$^-3$	$^-4$	$^-5$

(b), (d)

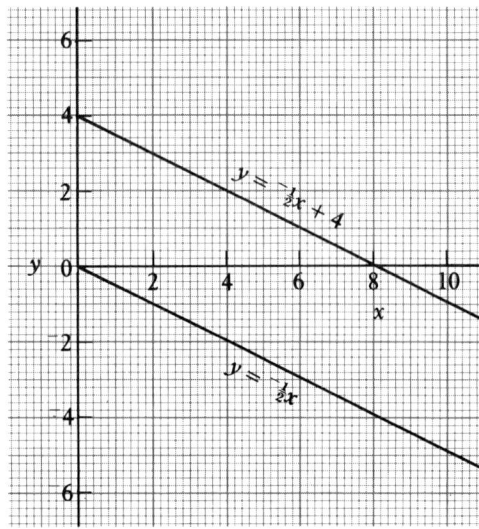

(c)

x	0	2	4	6	8	10
y	4	3	2	1	0	$^-1$

(e) (i) $^-\frac{1}{2}$ (ii) 4

E Fitting a linear formula

E1 (a) 0·5 (b) 2·4
(c) $B = 0·5l + 2·4$
(d) The numbers in the table do fit.

E2 (a)

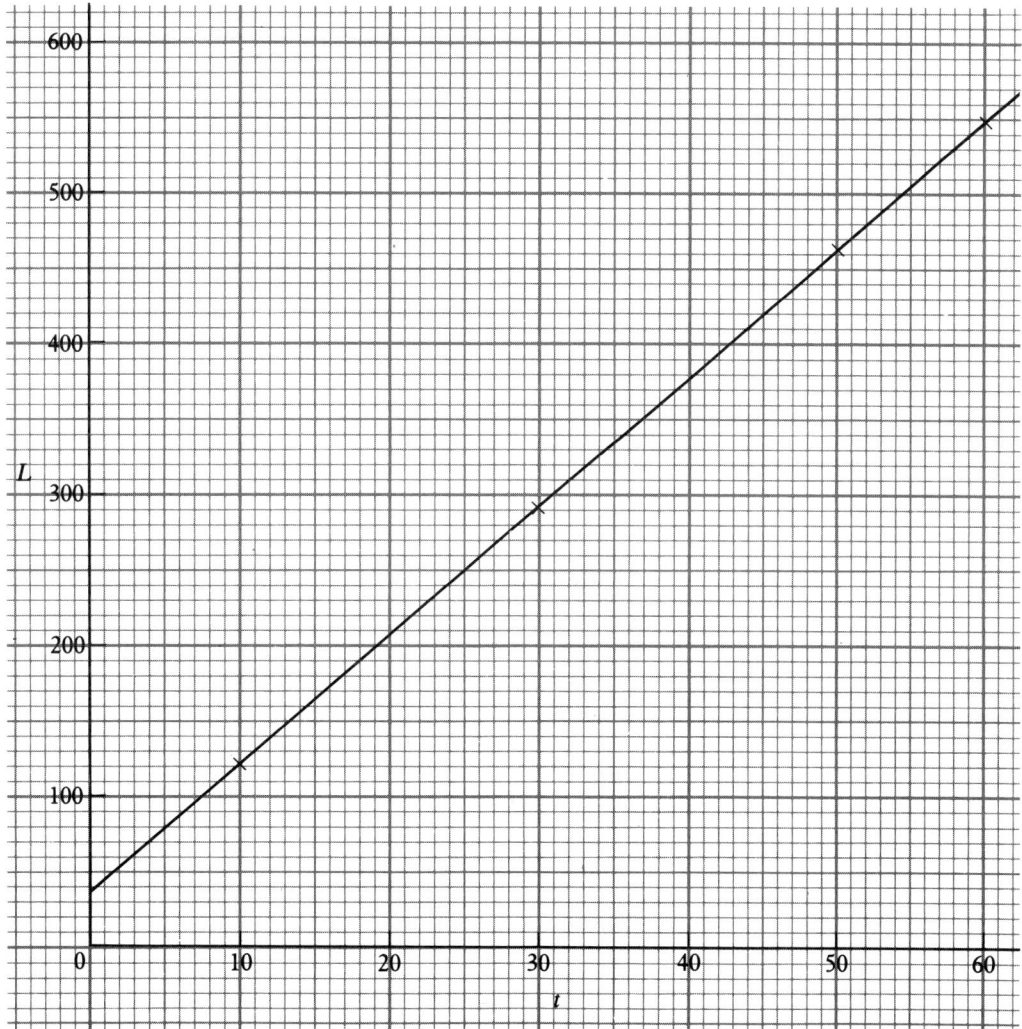

(b) 8·5 (c) 35
(d) $L = 8·5t + 35$
(e) The numbers in the table do fit.

E3 (a), (b)

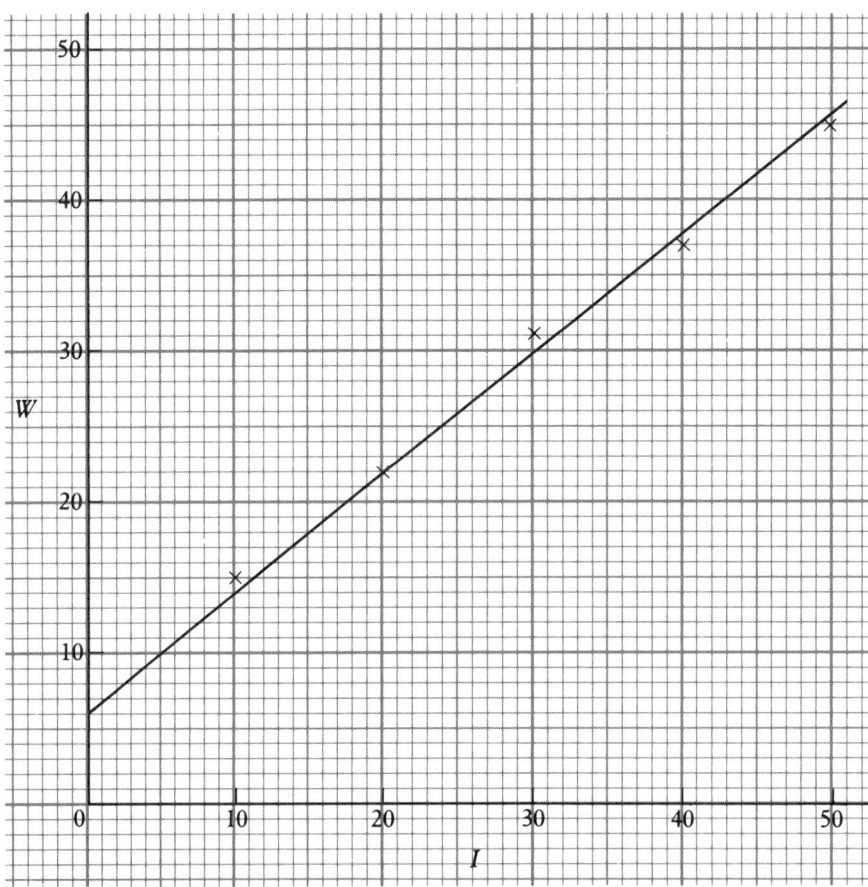

(c) Gradient = 0·81 (approx.),
intercept = 6·0 (approx.)
$$W = 0·81I + 6·0$$

E4 (a)

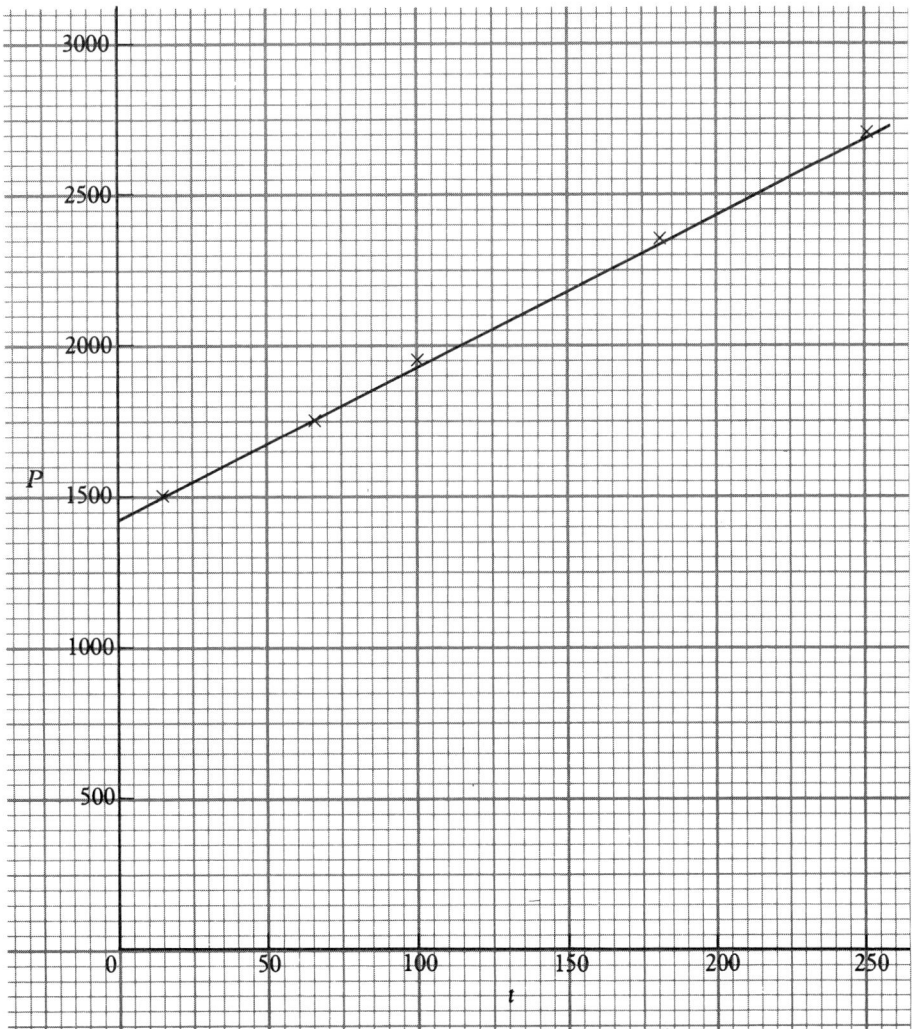

(b) $p = 5 \cdot 2t + 1400$ (approx.)
(c) $p = 3500$ (approx.)
(d) $880\,°C$ (approx.)

E5 (a)

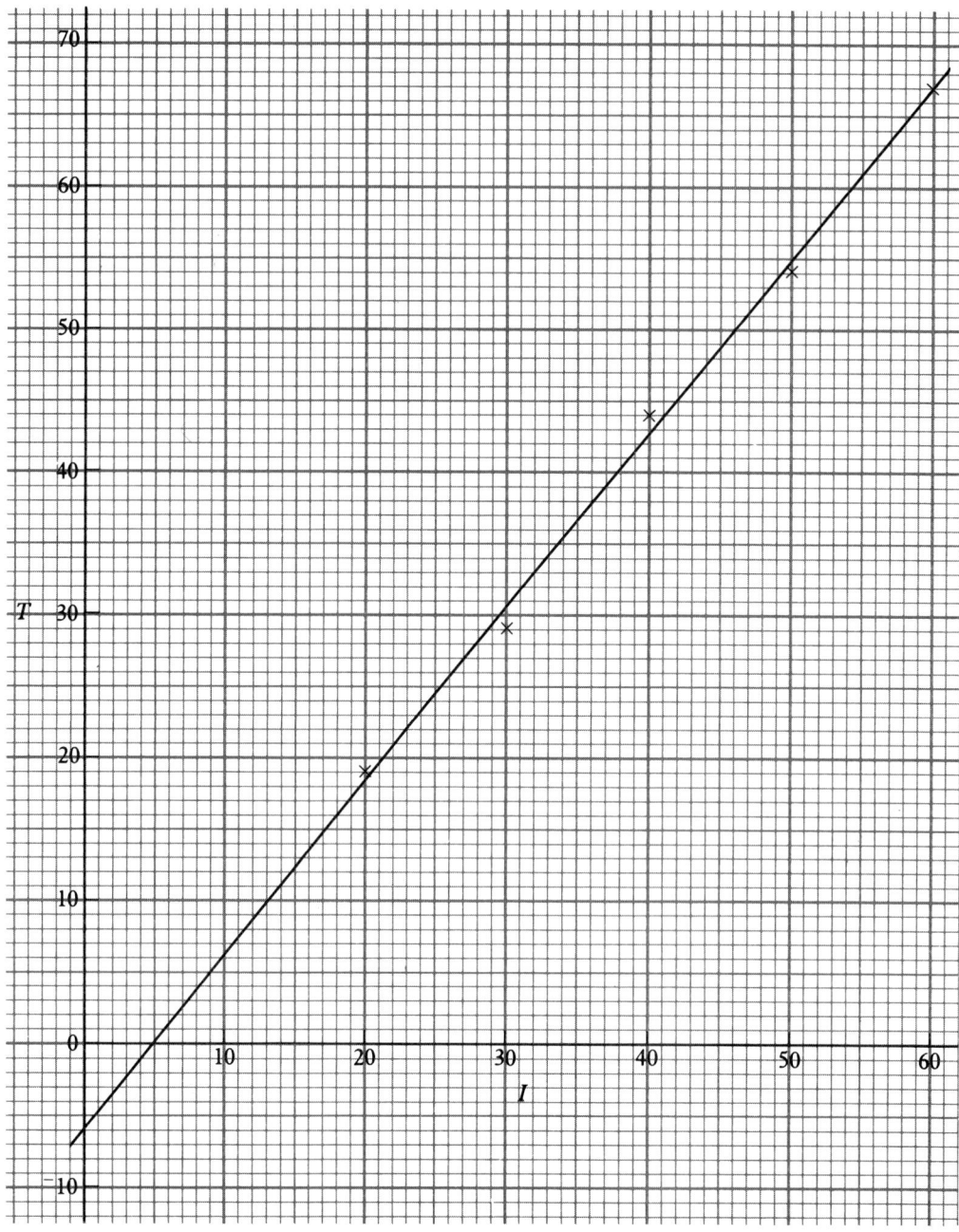

(b) $T = 1{\cdot}2I - 6{\cdot}0$ (approx.)
(c) About 5 m.p.h.

F   Re-arranging equations into gradient–intercept form

F1 (a) $y = 4x + 7$ (b) $y = 3x - 2$
     (c) $y = {}^-x + 6$ (d) $y = {}^-6x + 5$

F2 (a) $y = {}^-3x + 4$ (b) $y = 4x + 6$
     (c) $y = {}^-2x + 10$ (d) $y = {}^-\frac{1}{3}x + 4$
     (e) $y = {}^-\frac{3}{4}x + 2$ (f) $y = x - 7$
     (g) $y = \frac{1}{2}x - 4\frac{1}{2}$ (h) $y = \frac{1}{4}x + \frac{5}{4}$
     (i) $y = \frac{2}{3}x - 5$ (j) $y = {}^-x + 3$
     (k) $y = \frac{5}{3}x + \frac{1}{3}$ (l) $y = \frac{4}{3}x - \frac{10}{3}$

If all you have is...   (pages 23–4)

This is the first of three short sections on geometrical constructions.

1

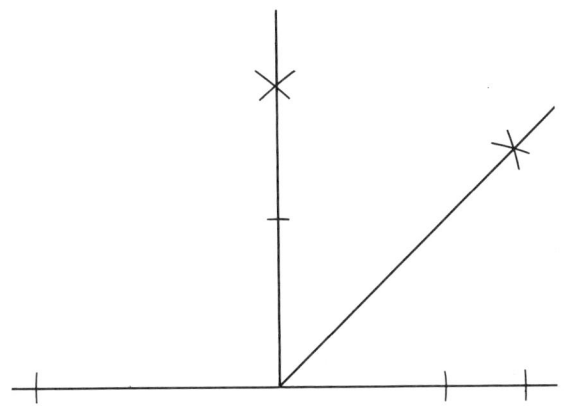

2

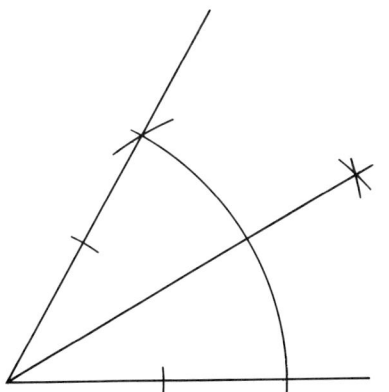

First construct a 60° angle (as on page 23); then bisect it.

3

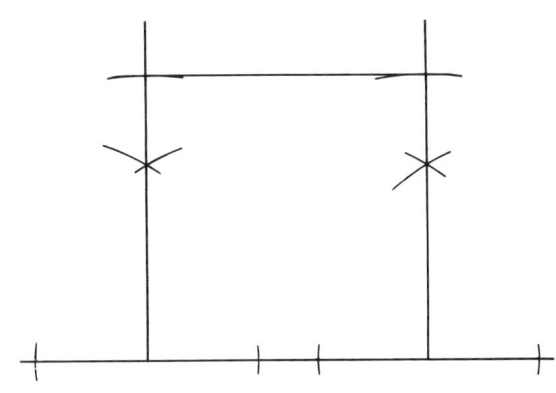

First draw two lines at right-angles, as in 1.

4

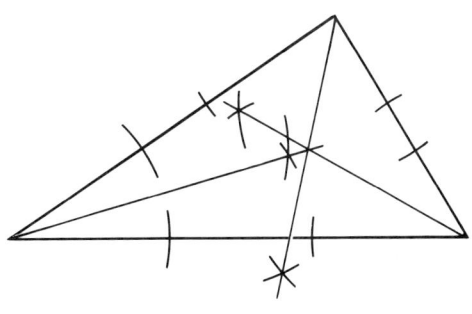

The three bisectors meet at a single point (the centre of the inscribed circle).

5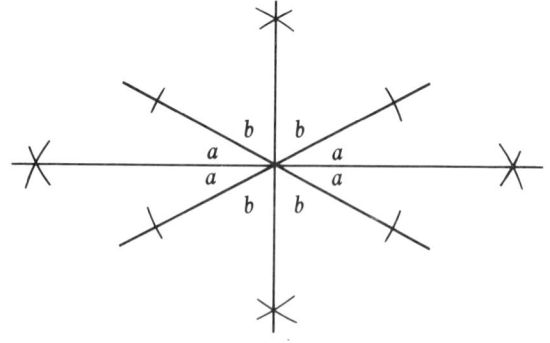

Opposite bisectors form a single straight line.
The two lines cross at right-angles.
$4(a + b) = 360$ so $a + b = 90$

6 This construction can become very unclear. The following diagram has been tidied up to show the essential features.

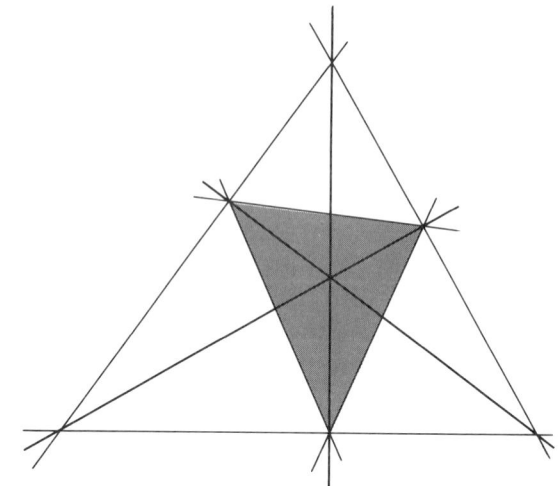

Able pupils could be asked to investigate the relationship between the angles of the newly formed large triangle and the angles of the original triangle.

3 Vectors

Some pupils may have met vectors before, in levels 3(e) and 4(e) of the booklet scheme, so for them this chapter may be a reminder. The chapter introduces displacement vectors, their representation by column vectors, and the use of the latter to describe translations.

A Displacement vectors
Answers to A1–A5 depend on accurate drawing. Pupils' answers can be expected to vary accordingly.

A1 (a), (b)

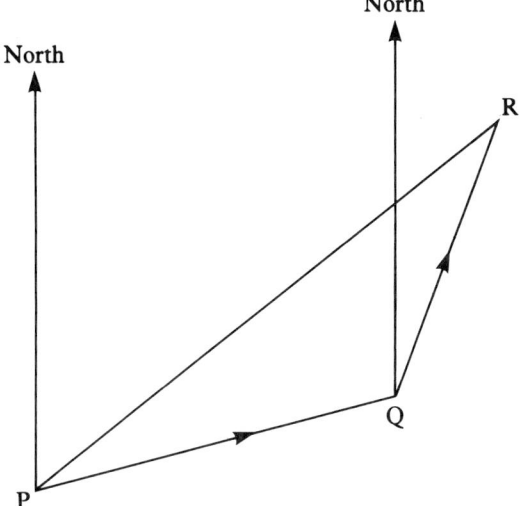

(c) Vector $\overrightarrow{PR}$ has length 80 km and bearing 051°.

A2 (a), (b)

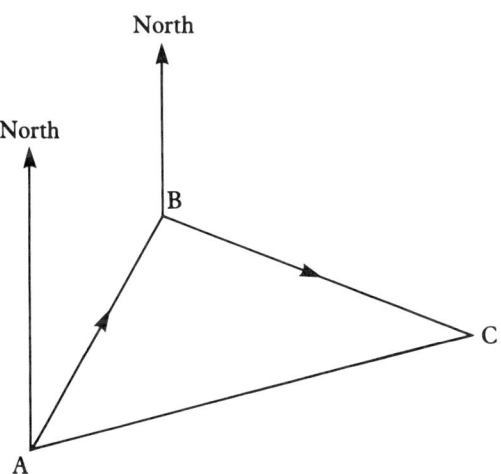

(c) Vector $\overrightarrow{AC}$ has length 62 km and bearing 076°.

A3

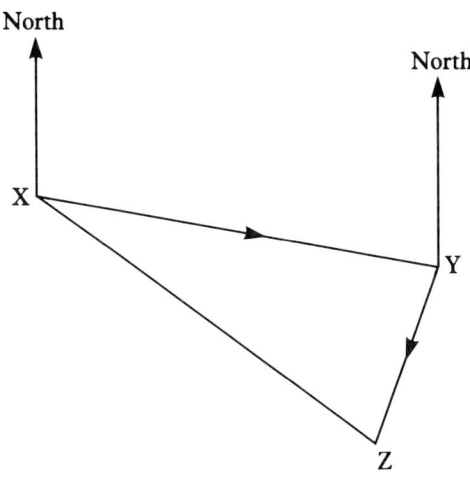

Vector $\overrightarrow{XY}$ has length 56 km and bearing 126°.

A4

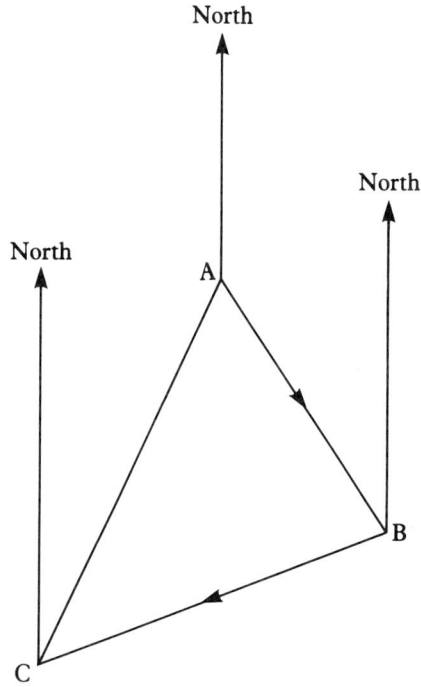

$\overrightarrow{CA}$ has length 55 km and bearing 026°.

A5

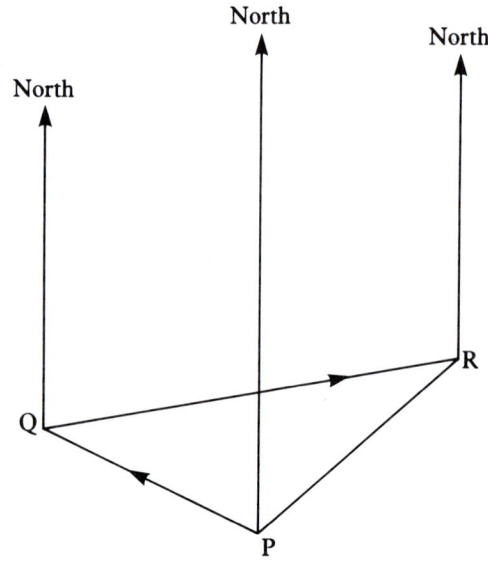

$\overrightarrow{RP}$ has length 36 km and bearing 229°.

★A6 (a) 250° (b) 310°
(c) (i) 020° (ii) 120°
(d) If the bearing of $\overrightarrow{AB}$ is $x°$ then the bearing of $\overrightarrow{BA}$ is
$x + 180°$ (if $x < 180$)
$x - 180°$ (if $x \geq 180$)

B Column vectors

B1 (a) $\begin{bmatrix} 4 \\ -2 \end{bmatrix}$ (b) $\begin{bmatrix} -2 \\ -4 \end{bmatrix}$ (c) $\begin{bmatrix} -3 \\ 4 \end{bmatrix}$
(d) $\begin{bmatrix} 3 \\ 1 \end{bmatrix}$ (e) $\begin{bmatrix} 3 \\ -3 \end{bmatrix}$ (f) $\begin{bmatrix} -4 \\ 4 \end{bmatrix}$
(g) $\begin{bmatrix} -5 \\ 0 \end{bmatrix}$ (h) $\begin{bmatrix} 0 \\ -4 \end{bmatrix}$ (i) $\begin{bmatrix} -3 \\ -2 \end{bmatrix}$

B2

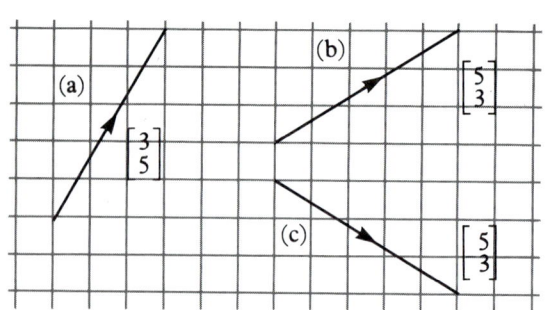

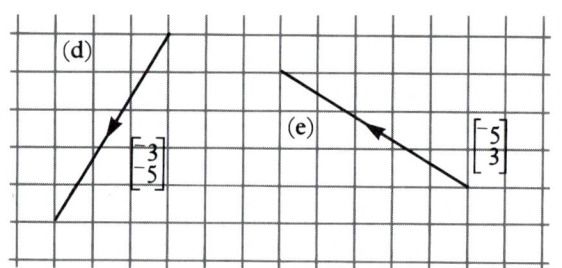

B3 $\overrightarrow{AB} = \overrightarrow{OP}$, $\overrightarrow{GH} = \overrightarrow{KL}$

B4 (a) $\begin{bmatrix} -4 \\ -5 \end{bmatrix}$ (b) $\begin{bmatrix} 1 \\ -4 \end{bmatrix}$ (c) $\begin{bmatrix} -5 \\ 2 \end{bmatrix}$
(d) $\begin{bmatrix} 3 \\ 4 \end{bmatrix}$ (e) $\begin{bmatrix} -2 \\ 0 \end{bmatrix}$ (f) $\begin{bmatrix} 0 \\ 5 \end{bmatrix}$
(g) $\begin{bmatrix} 0 \\ -7 \end{bmatrix}$ (h) $\begin{bmatrix} 6 \\ 0 \end{bmatrix}$ (i) $\begin{bmatrix} -6 \\ 7 \end{bmatrix}$
(j) $\begin{bmatrix} 2 \\ -8 \end{bmatrix}$

C Adding vectors

C1 (a) $\begin{bmatrix} 1 \\ 2 \end{bmatrix}$, $\begin{bmatrix} 6 \\ 0 \end{bmatrix}$, $\begin{bmatrix} 4 \\ 1 \end{bmatrix}$, $\begin{bmatrix} 0 \\ 3 \end{bmatrix}$
(b) $\begin{bmatrix} 1 \\ 2 \end{bmatrix} + \begin{bmatrix} 6 \\ 0 \end{bmatrix} + \begin{bmatrix} 4 \\ 1 \end{bmatrix} + \begin{bmatrix} 0 \\ 3 \end{bmatrix} = \begin{bmatrix} 11 \\ 6 \end{bmatrix}$
(c) This is the correct column vector for $\overrightarrow{PT}$.

C2 $\begin{bmatrix} 3 \\ -5 \end{bmatrix}$

C3 (b) $\begin{bmatrix} -3 \\ -4 \end{bmatrix} + \begin{bmatrix} -2 \\ 6 \end{bmatrix} = \begin{bmatrix} -5 \\ 2 \end{bmatrix}$

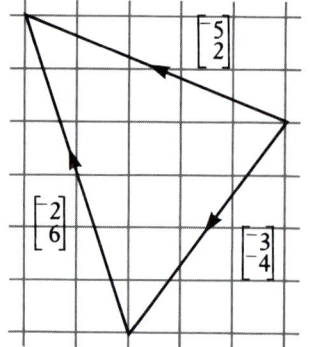

(c) $\begin{bmatrix} 3 \\ -7 \end{bmatrix} + \begin{bmatrix} -5 \\ 2 \end{bmatrix} = \begin{bmatrix} -2 \\ -5 \end{bmatrix}$

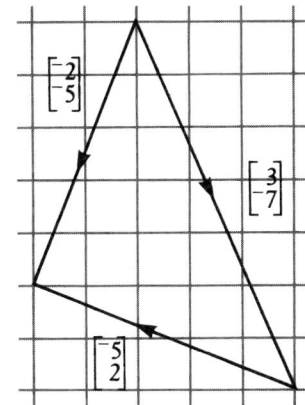

C4 (a) $\begin{bmatrix} 2 \\ 6 \end{bmatrix}$ (b) $\begin{bmatrix} -1 \\ 4 \end{bmatrix}$ (c) $\begin{bmatrix} -4 \\ -7 \end{bmatrix}$
(d) $\begin{bmatrix} -5 \\ -3 \end{bmatrix}$ (e) $\begin{bmatrix} 4 \\ 0 \end{bmatrix}$ (f) $\begin{bmatrix} -4 \\ -9 \end{bmatrix}$

C5 (a) $\begin{bmatrix} 9 \\ 7 \end{bmatrix}$ (b) $\begin{bmatrix} 8 \\ 2 \end{bmatrix}$
(c) $\begin{bmatrix} -3 \\ 10 \end{bmatrix}$ (d) $\begin{bmatrix} 6 \\ -5 \end{bmatrix}$

D Translations

D1 $\begin{bmatrix} 5 \\ 1 \end{bmatrix}$

D2 $\begin{bmatrix} 5 \\ 2 \end{bmatrix}$

D3

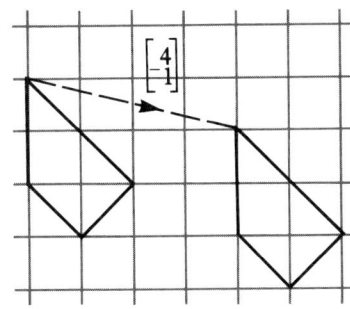

D4 (a) $\begin{bmatrix} 9 \\ 0 \end{bmatrix}$ (b) $\begin{bmatrix} 5 \\ -2 \end{bmatrix}$ (c) $\begin{bmatrix} 0 \\ -7 \end{bmatrix}$ (d) $\begin{bmatrix} -7 \\ 4 \end{bmatrix}$
(e) $\begin{bmatrix} -2 \\ -4 \end{bmatrix}$ (f) $\begin{bmatrix} 2 \\ 3 \end{bmatrix}$ (g) $\begin{bmatrix} 2 \\ -2 \end{bmatrix}$ (h) $\begin{bmatrix} -2 \\ 2 \end{bmatrix}$
(i) $\begin{bmatrix} 6 \\ 0 \end{bmatrix}$ (j) $\begin{bmatrix} -9 \\ 0 \end{bmatrix}$

D5 (a) $\begin{bmatrix} 1 \\ 3 \end{bmatrix}$ (b) $\begin{bmatrix} 4 \\ 2 \end{bmatrix}$
(c) $\begin{bmatrix} 1 \\ 3 \end{bmatrix} + \begin{bmatrix} 4 \\ 2 \end{bmatrix} = \begin{bmatrix} 5 \\ 5 \end{bmatrix}$
This is the column vector of the translation F to C.

E Translation symmetry

E1 (a) It fits over flower I. (b) $\begin{bmatrix} -1 \\ -3 \end{bmatrix}$
(c) These are an infinite number of possible answers. Here are some of them:
$\begin{bmatrix} -2 \\ -1 \end{bmatrix} \begin{bmatrix} -4 \\ -2 \end{bmatrix} \begin{bmatrix} 1 \\ -2 \end{bmatrix} \begin{bmatrix} -1 \\ -3 \end{bmatrix} \begin{bmatrix} -3 \\ -4 \end{bmatrix}$
$\begin{bmatrix} 2 \\ -4 \end{bmatrix} \begin{bmatrix} 0 \\ -5 \end{bmatrix} \begin{bmatrix} -2 \\ -6 \end{bmatrix} \begin{bmatrix} 3 \\ -6 \end{bmatrix} \begin{bmatrix} 2 \\ 1 \end{bmatrix}$
$\begin{bmatrix} 4 \\ 2 \end{bmatrix} \begin{bmatrix} 1 \\ 3 \end{bmatrix} \begin{bmatrix} 3 \\ 4 \end{bmatrix} \begin{bmatrix} 5 \\ 0 \end{bmatrix} \begin{bmatrix} -5 \\ 0 \end{bmatrix}$
$\begin{bmatrix} 2 \\ 6 \end{bmatrix} \begin{bmatrix} -3 \\ 1 \end{bmatrix} \begin{bmatrix} 3 \\ -1 \end{bmatrix} \begin{bmatrix} 7 \\ -4 \end{bmatrix} \begin{bmatrix} -7 \\ 4 \end{bmatrix} \ldots$

E2 All four patterns have translation symmetry. There are many different possible vectors in each case. Each individual pupil's answers will need to be checked.

Pattern (a) has reflection symmetry as well. Patterns (c) and (d) have both reflection and rotation symmetry.

See diagram on page 22.

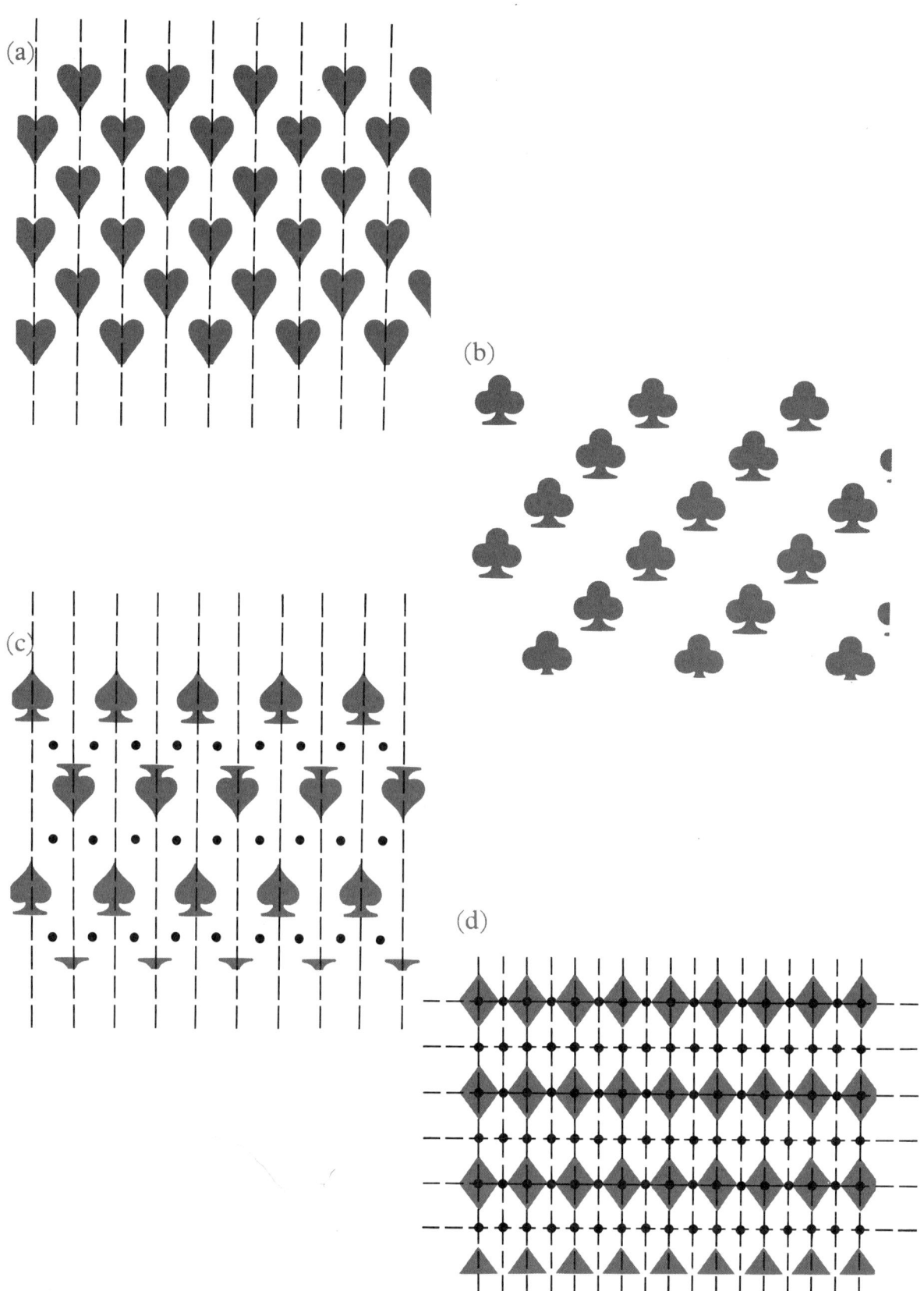

22

Algebra review (1)

This is the first of three sets of questions on some of the main ideas and techniques of algebra introduced earlier in the course.

1. (a) 82 black balls (b) $b = 4r + 2$
   (c) $r = \dfrac{b - 2}{4}$

2. $c + vr$

3. (a) $8a + 4b$ (b) $4ab + b^2$

4. (a) $8a - 5$ (b) $6 + 5x$ (c) $2 - 4s$
   (d) $2a^2 - 2a + 4$
   (e) Impossible to simplify (f) $^{-}3 - 4y$

5. (a) $3x - 3$ (b) $4 + 3a$
   (c) $y + 3$ (d) $15 - 4s$
   (e) $10t - 6$ (f) $2 - 4u$

6. $b + c - a$

7. (a) $x = 7$ (b) $x = 7$
   (c) $x = 5$ (d) $x = 51$
   (e) $x = 75$ (f) $x = 84$

8. (a) $xy + 3x + 5y + 15$
   (b) $x^2 + 8x + 15$

   (c) $x^2 - 9x + 14$
   (d) $x^2 - 13x + 36$
   (e) $2x^2 - x - 3$
   (f) $10x^2 - 7x - 12$

9. (a) The difference is always 4.
   (b) (i) $n + 2,\ n + 3,\ n + 4,\ n + 5$
       (ii) $n(n + 5)$ and $(n + 1)(n + 4)$
       (iii) $n(n + 5) = n^2 + 5n$
       $(n + 1)(n + 4) = n^2 + 5n + 4$
       So the product of the second and fifth numbers will always be 4 more than the product of the first and sixth numbers.

10. (a) $x = \dfrac{y - a}{b}$ (b) $s = at - m$
    (c) $m = at - s$ (d) $u = wc + v$
    (e) $v = u - wc$ (f) $x = a(r + e)$

11. $10\,°\text{C}$

4 Percentage (1)

Percentages are used to compare proportions. The chapter extends this work to the comparison of proportions derived from data presented in two-way tables.

A Comparison

A1 UK 51·3%; Republic of Ireland 49·8% (both to 1 d.p.)

A2 (a)

Land use	UK	Ireland
Arable, etc.	28·9%	15·1%
Pasture	48·1%	55·5%
Forest	8·4%	3·0%
Other	14·6%	26·4%

(b)

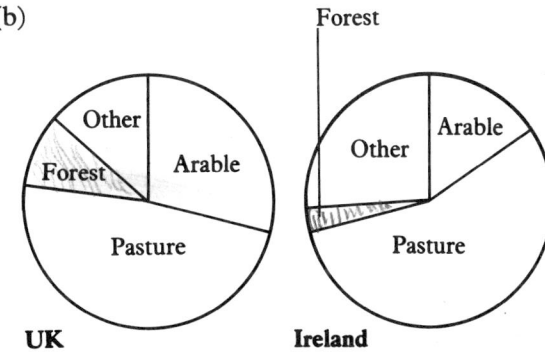

UK   Ireland

23

A3 (a)

1979
Conservative	44·9%
Labour	37·7%
Liberal	14·1%
Others	3·3%

1983
Conservative	43·5%
Labour	28·3%
Liberal/SDP	26·0%
Others	2·2%

(b) Pie charts for 1979 and 1983 showing Others, Conservative, Liberal (Liberal/SDP in 1983), and Labour.

B Two-way tables

B1 23·6, 3·2, 23·4, 4·8 million, respectively

B2 U.K.
	Male	Female	Total
Under 65	42·9%	42·5%	85·4%
Over 65	5·8%	8·7%	14·5%
	48·7%	51·2%	100% (55·0 million)

B3 ITALY
	Male	Female	Total
Under 65	43·3%	43·3%	86·6%
Over 65	5·6%	7·9%	13·5%
	48·9%	51·2%	100% (57·1 million)

B4 The tables are quite similar. In both countries the proportion of men and women under 65 is about equal but there are about 3 women for every 2 men in the over 65 age-group.
The biggest difference between the two countries is that Italy has a slightly smaller percentage of its population over 65.

B5 ITALY
	Male	Female	Total
Under 65	50%	50%	100% (49·4 million)
Over 65	41·6%	58·4%	100% (7·7 million)

The table is similar to that of the UK.

B6 ITALY
	Male	Female
Under 65	88·5%	84·6%
Over 65	11·5%	15·4%
	100% (27·9 million)	100% (29·2 million)

B7 (a) UK (b) UK (c) UK (d) Italy
Correct answers here are not sufficient. Pupils should be asked for the locations of the evidence!

C Interpreting accident statistics

This section will need considerable discussion.

C1 (a)
	Slight	Serious	Fatal	Total
1st quarter	67·7%	30·5%	1·8%	100% (1446)
2nd quarter	66·4%	31·1%	2·5%	100% (1570)
3rd quarter	68·8%	29·2%	2·0%	100% (1655)
4th quarter	66·6%	31·0%	2·4%	100% (1779)

(b)
	Slight	Serious	Fatal
1st quarter	22·5%	22·4%	18·4%
2nd quarter	24·0%	24·9%	27·7%
3rd quarter	26·2%	24·6%	23·4%
4th quarter	27·3%	28·1%	30·5%
Total	100% (4344)	100% (1965)	100% (141)

(c) The explanation is given at the bottom of page 42 of the pupil's book.

C2 (a) 43·5% (b) 7·7%
(c) The explanation is given at the bottom of page 42 of the pupil's book.

C3 (a) It would be fairer to work out the number of accidents per kilometre of road. This is shown in the following table:

Road	Accidents per km (to 2 d.p.)
A13	5·44
A127	4·47
A128	3·94
A130	3·65
A133	3·55
A12	2·66
A414	2·55
A120	2·46
A131	1·86
A604	1·51
M11	1·31

(b) The chief factor not allowed for is probably the amount of traffic actually using each road.

C4

	Serious/fatal	Slight	Total
Wearing belt	20·6%	79·4%	100% (864)
Not wearing	29·7%	70·3%	100% (2138)

The data refers only to those people who were in accidents and received a reported injury.

Of these people, a higher percentage of those not wearing a seat belt than those who were wearing a seat belt were seriously injured. This suggests that wearing a seat belt helps to prevent serious injury.

However, there is no data for those who were involved in accidents and received no injury.

C5 Drivers who have been drinking are only a small percentage of all drivers and so even if they were just as safe as other drivers they would be involved in only a small percentage of accidents.

5 Mappings

This chapter takes up the threads of earlier work in the course on reflection, rotation and translation. The last section presents work in which all three of these kinds of mapping may be involved, and explores examples of the combination of mappings.

A Reflection

A1 (a)

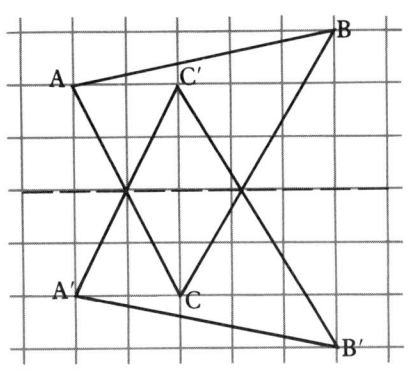

(b)

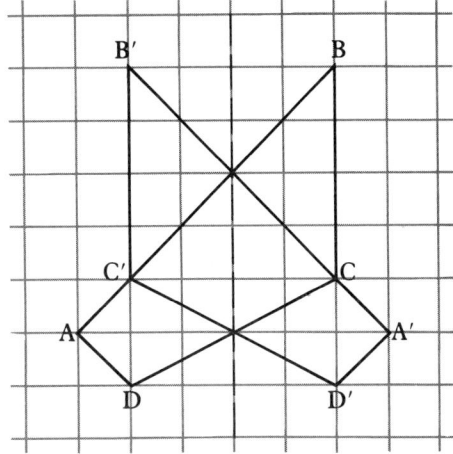

(c)

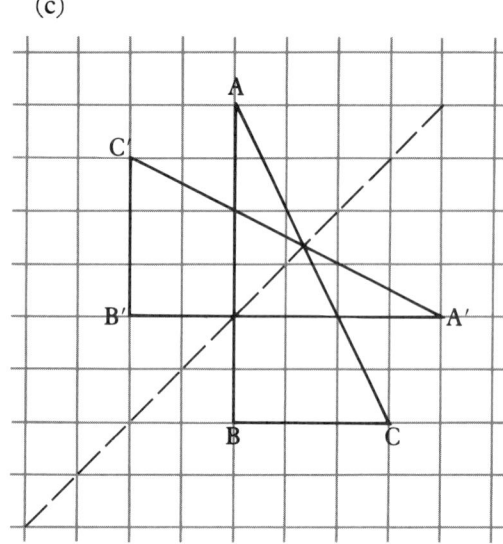

A2 (a)

Object	Image
(7, 3)	(3, 7)
(2, 4)	(4, 2)
(0, 4)	(4, 0)
(⁻2, 1)	(1, ⁻2)
(⁻1, 6)	(6, ⁻1)

(b) The x and y coordinates swop over; i.e. the image of a general point (p, q) is (q, p).

(c) (i) (19, 13) (ii) (18, ⁻6) (iii) (⁻10, ⁻4) (iv) (b, a)

A3 (a)

Object	Image
(4, 3)	(6, 3)
(2, 5)	(8, 5)
(1, ⁻2)	(9, ⁻2)
(7, 6)	(3, 6)
(5, 1)	(5, 1)

(b) x coordinate of object + x coordinate of image = 10

(c) (i) (7, 20) (ii) (4, ⁻8) (iii) (10, 7) (iv) (11, 5) (v) (⁻3, 4)

A4 $(10 - a, b)$

B 180° rotation

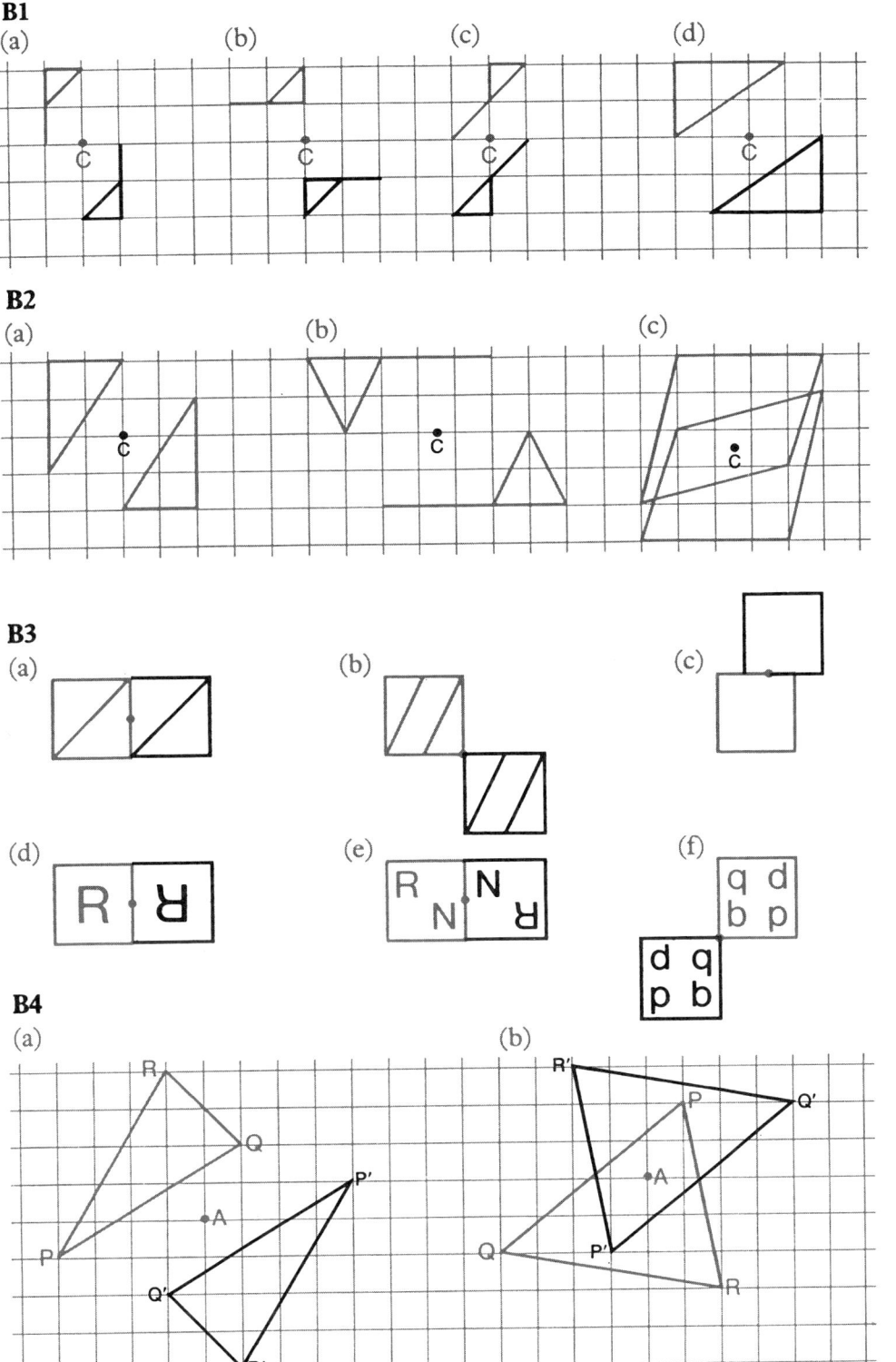

C 90° rotation

C1
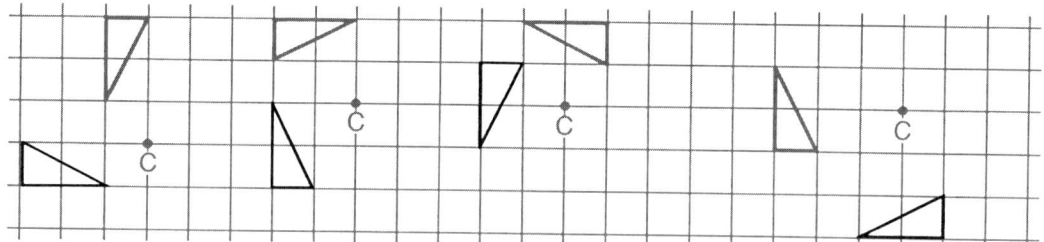

C2
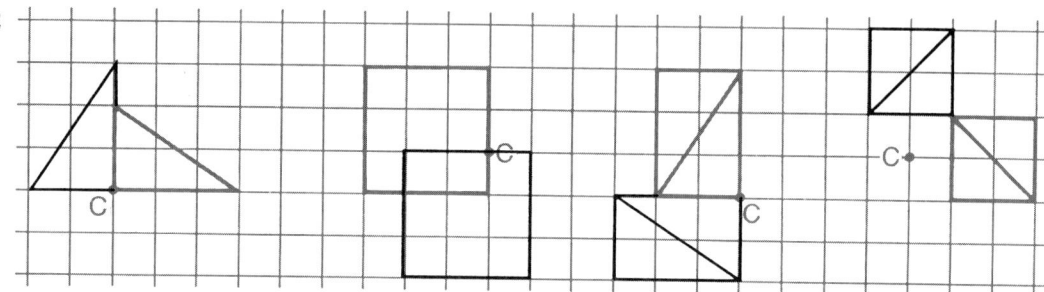

C3
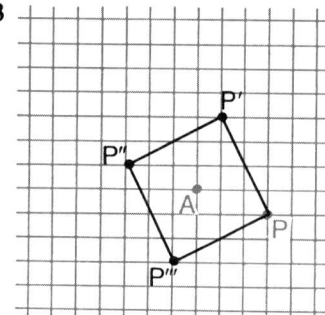

C4
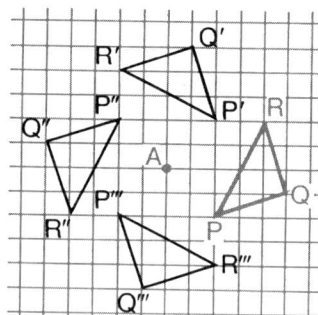

C5
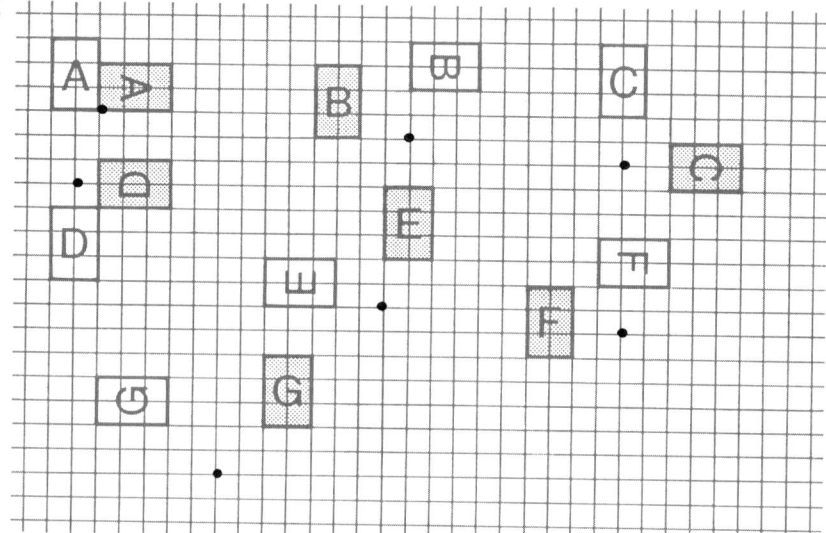

C3 (d) PP'P"P''' is a square and A is at the centre of the square.

C4 (d) 4-fold rotation symmetry

D Translation

D1 (a) $\begin{bmatrix} 4 \\ -1 \end{bmatrix}$ (b) $\begin{bmatrix} -5 \\ -2 \end{bmatrix}$ (c) $\begin{bmatrix} -6 \\ 2 \end{bmatrix}$
(d) $\begin{bmatrix} 0 \\ -4 \end{bmatrix}$ (e) $\begin{bmatrix} 5 \\ 0 \end{bmatrix}$ (f) $\begin{bmatrix} 3 \\ -1 \end{bmatrix}$
(g) $\begin{bmatrix} 0 \\ 3 \end{bmatrix}$

F4

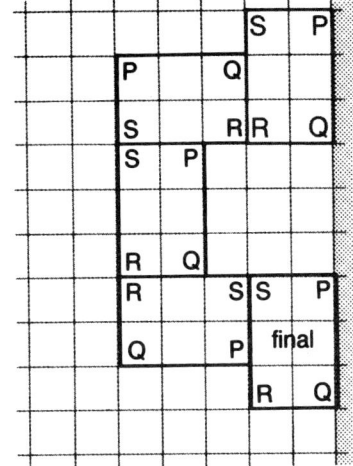

E Congruence

E1 (a) The tracing will fit over triangle 2 but not over triangle 3.
(b) Triangle 2, clockwise; triangle 3, anticlockwise

E2 Directly congruent: a, b, d, g
Oppositely congruent: c, e, f, h

F Mappings

F1 (a) Triangles 3, 5, 7
(b) Triangles 2, 4, 6, 8
(c) (i) Rotation of 90° clockwise, centre (0, 0)
    (ii) Rotation of 180°, centre (0, 0)
    (iii) Reflection in $y = {}^-x$
    (iv) Reflection in the y-axis

F2 (a) Reflection in the x-axis
(b) Rotation of 90° anticlockwise, centre (0, 0)
(c) Reflection in $y = x$

F3

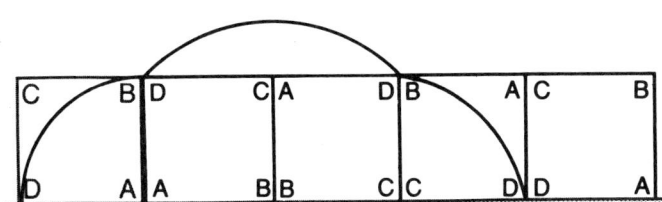

F5 Here is one possible solution.
The rotations used were:
   90° anticlockwise about B,
   180° anticlockwise about A,
   90° anticlockwise about D,
   90° clockwise about C,
   90° anticlockwise about D.

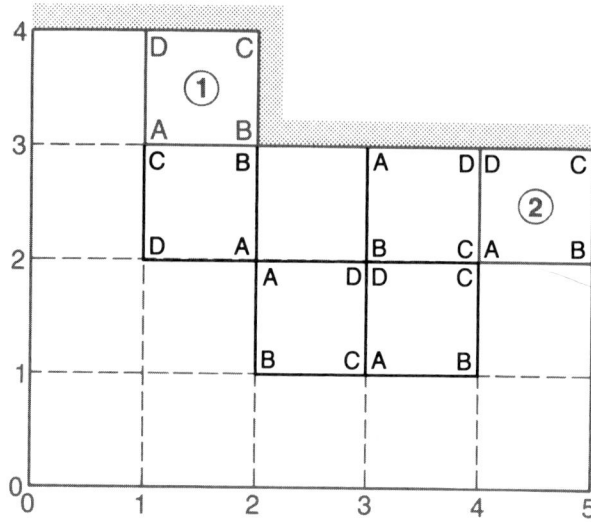

Pupils could be asked various supplementary questions such as:
   Can you find the fewest number of rotations? (3)
   What practical difficulties would there be?
   What orientations are possible in the final position? (Presumably the door is either on side AB or AD.)

F6

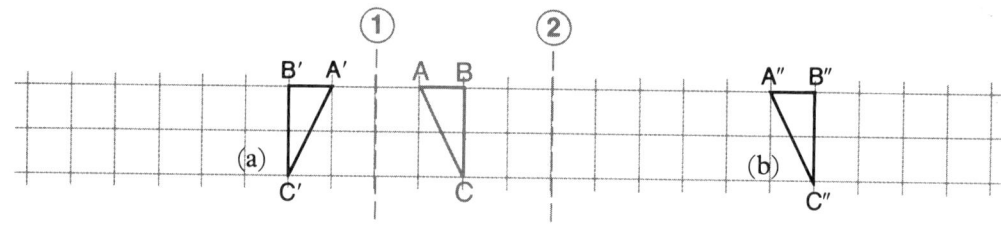

(c) Translation with vector $\begin{bmatrix} 8 \\ 0 \end{bmatrix}$

F7

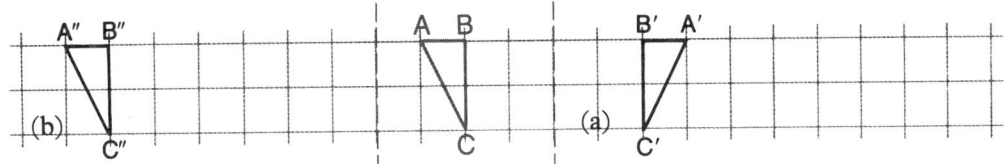

(c) Translation with vector $\begin{bmatrix} -8 \\ 0 \end{bmatrix}$

F8

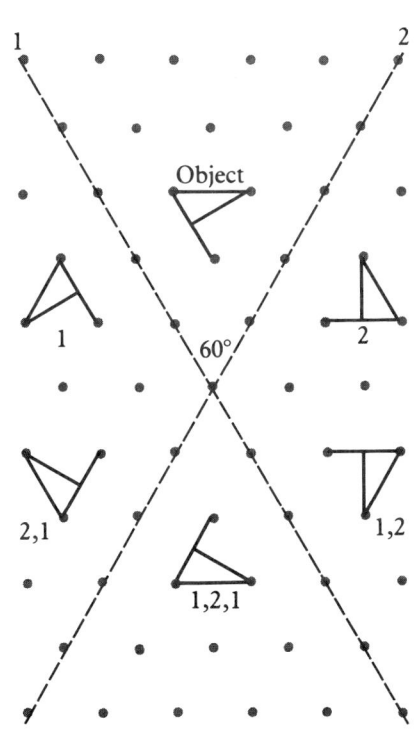

*F9 (a)

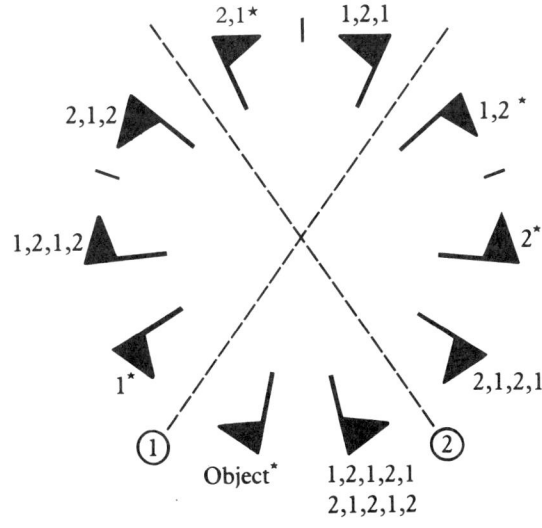

(b) You only see four images (marked with asterisks in the diagram above).
Image 1,2,1, for example, is not seen because its 'object' 1,2 doesn't exist.

6 Investigations (1)

1.
Number of bricks	1	2	3	4	5	6
Number of rectangles	1	3	6	10	15	21

The *increase* goes up by 1 each time

In going from a diagram with, say, 4 bricks to the diagram with 5 bricks, there are 5 *extra* rectangles not counted before.

An alternative approach is to count as in the example below

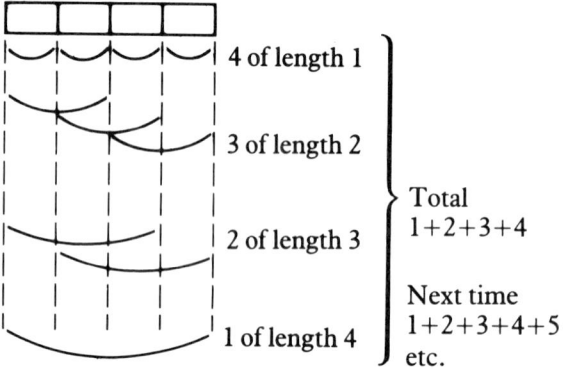

4 of length 1

3 of length 2

2 of length 3

1 of length 4

Total
1+2+3+4

Next time
1+2+3+4+5
etc.

Able pupils could be asked to try to find the algebraic formula for the number of rectangles when there are n bricks:

$$\frac{n(n+1)}{2}$$

2 The pattern of folds develops in a very predictable way which pupils can be asked to try to explain.

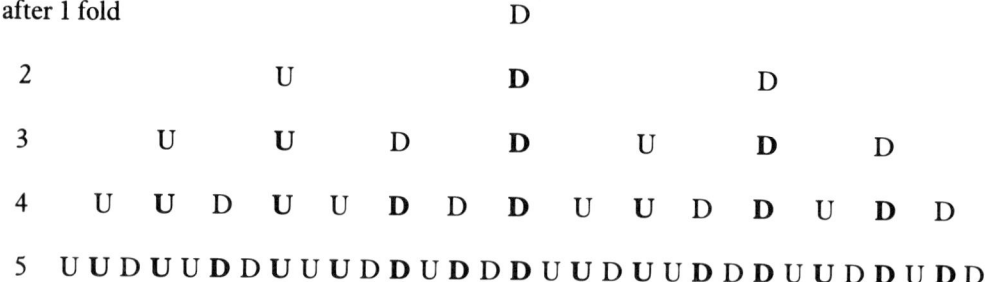

after 1 fold   D

2   U   D   D

3   U   U   D   D   U   D   D

4   U U D U U D D D U U D D U D D

5   U U D U U D D U U D D U D D D U U D U U D D D U U D D U D D

There is an opportunity to extend the task so that a pupil may be asked what the pattern would be after, say, 10 folds (if that many were possible); or what if the strip were folded in thirds each time?

3

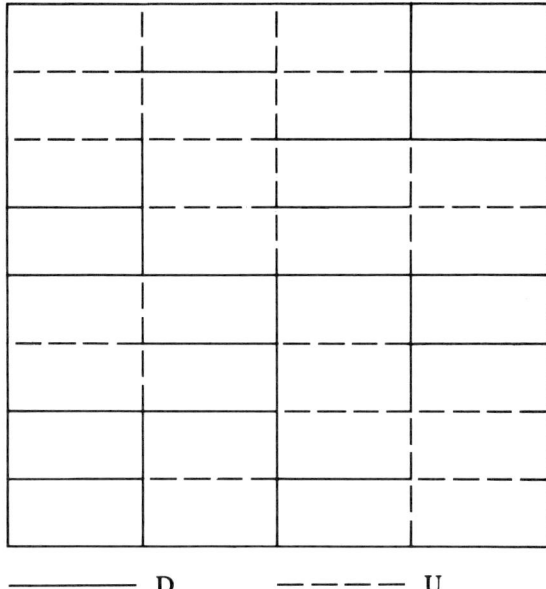

———— D – – – – U

The pattern of folds develops in a predictable way. The arrangement after 5 folds is shown in the diagram.
Pupils could be asked to predict the pattern after 6 or 7 folds.

Review 1

1 Stretching and enlargement

1.1 1·22 (to 3 s.f.)

1.2 (a) 3·24 (b) 2940 cm² (both to 3 s.f.)

1.3 486 cm²

1.4 11·84 cm²

1.5 (a) Scale factor 0·7, since the area factor is the square of the scale factor and $0·7^2 = 0·49$.
(b) Scale factor 0·6, since $0·6^2 = 0·36$.

2 Linear relationships

2.1 (a) $\frac{3}{2}$ (b) $^-\frac{1}{3}$ (c) $\frac{1}{2}$ (d) $\frac{1}{5}$
(e) $^-1$ (f) $^-3$

2.2 (a) $\frac{2}{3}$ (b) $^-\frac{1}{2}$ (c) 1 (d) $\frac{6}{5}$ (e) $^-2$
(f) $\frac{9}{5}$

2.3 (i) $y = \frac{1}{3}x$ (ii) $y = \frac{1}{3}x + 1$
(iii) $y = \frac{1}{3}x - 2$

2.4 (a) (i) 3 (ii) $^-5$ (b) (i) 2 (ii) 6
(c) (i) $^-4$ (ii) 10   (d) (i) $^-2$ (ii) 12

33

2.5 (a) $-\frac{1}{2}$
(b) (i) $y = -\frac{1}{2}x$ (ii) $y = -\frac{1}{2}x + 3$
(iii) $y = -\frac{1}{2}x - 1$

2.6 (a) 0·6 (b) $y = 0·6x + 1·4$

2.7 (a)

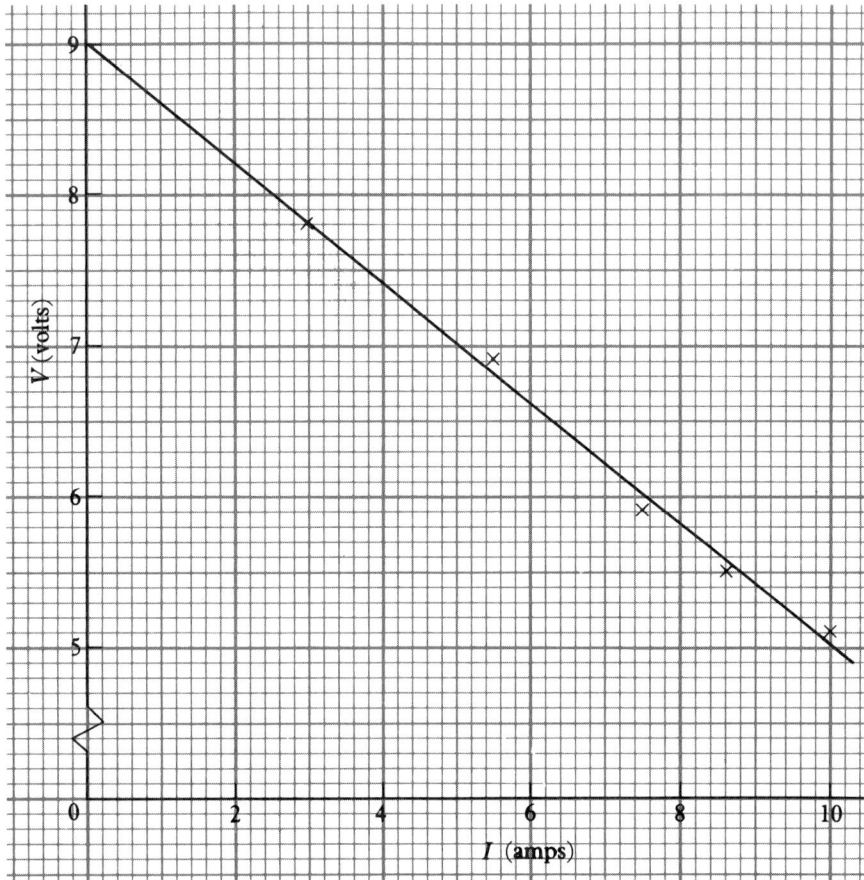

(b) $V = -0·40\,I + 9·0$ (approx.)

3 Vectors

3.1

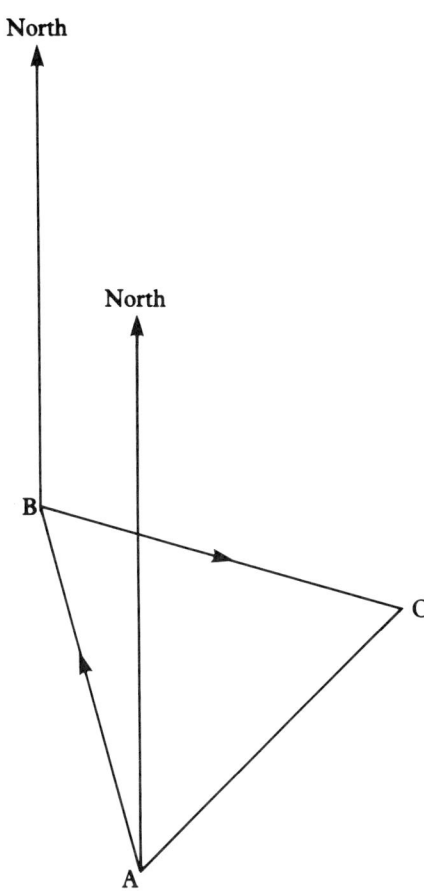

$\overrightarrow{AC}$ has length 50 km and bearing 045°. (Pupils could be asked to explain how this particular question could be done geometrically.)

3.2 (a) $\begin{bmatrix} -2 \\ -2 \end{bmatrix}$ (b) $\begin{bmatrix} 5 \\ -5 \end{bmatrix}$ (c) $\begin{bmatrix} -5 \\ -4 \end{bmatrix}$

3.3 (a) $\begin{bmatrix} 4 \\ 2 \end{bmatrix} \begin{bmatrix} 3 \\ -5 \end{bmatrix} \begin{bmatrix} -4 \\ -4 \end{bmatrix} \begin{bmatrix} -5 \\ 0 \end{bmatrix} \begin{bmatrix} -3 \\ 4 \end{bmatrix} \begin{bmatrix} 0 \\ 5 \end{bmatrix} \begin{bmatrix} 5 \\ -2 \end{bmatrix}$

(b) $\begin{bmatrix} 0 \\ 0 \end{bmatrix}$

(c) The total change of position for the journey is zero both horizontally and vertically because the journey starts and finishes at A.

4 Percentage (1)

4.1 (a)
Russia	5%
France	10%
Italy	5%
Serbia	10%
Belgium	1%
UK	5%
Austria	10%
Germany	10%
Turkey	5%

(b) 5·6% (c) 9·2%

(d) They were the opposing sides of the First World War.

4.2 No, this is not a fair conclusion as can be seen by looking at the table horizontally. Of the 527 given the drug, only 60% caught the disease; whereas of the 183 mice not given the drug, 74% caught the disease. This seems to suggest that the drug had some effect.

5 Mappings

5.1 (a), (b)

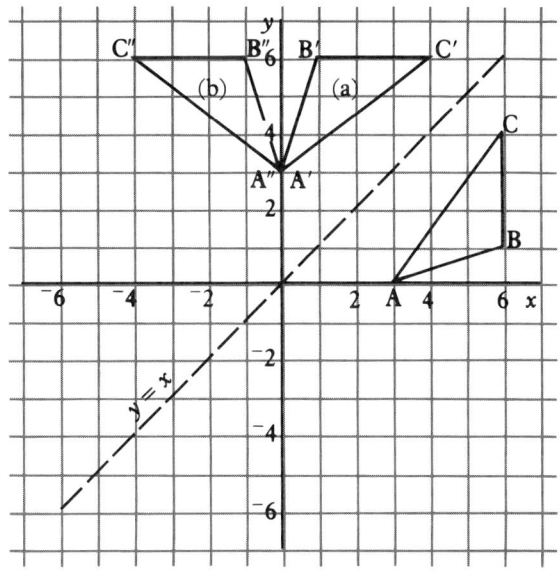

(c) Rotation of 90° anticlockwise, centre (0,0)

5.2

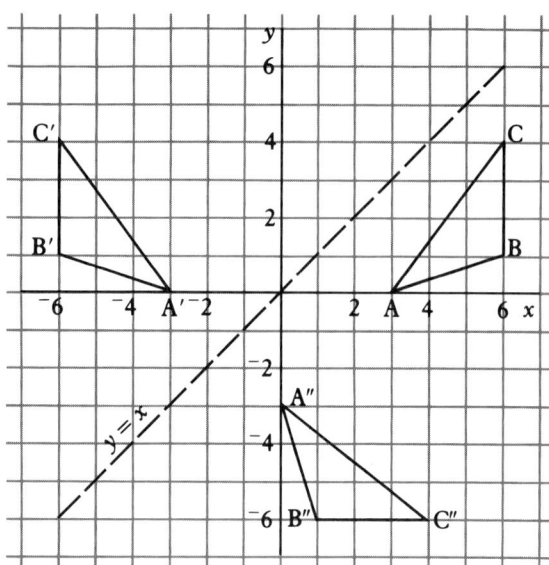

Rotation of 90° clockwise, centre (0,0)

5.3 The door will not shut because there is no 'clearance' to allow the leading edge of the door to miss the first edge of of the wall.

7 TV programmes survey

This is intended as a class activity. The class may be split up into groups to work on different channels. What will become evident – and this is an important part of the activity – is that people will differ about the classification of individual programmes, and there is no universally agreed 'right answer' for the percentage breakdown. This may worry some pupils, but it is an important point nevertheless.

If all you have is ... (page 67)

1

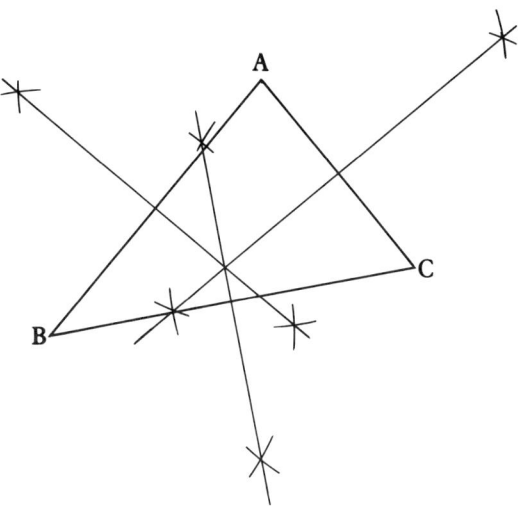

The three perpendicular bisectors meet at a single point (the centre of the circumscribed circle).

3

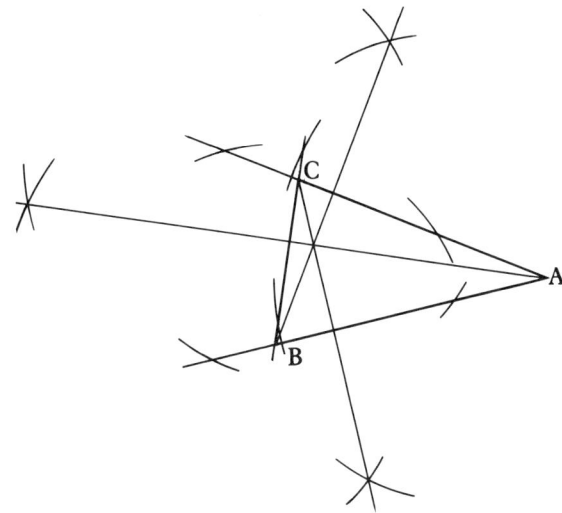

The three altitudes meet at a single point (the orthocentre).

2

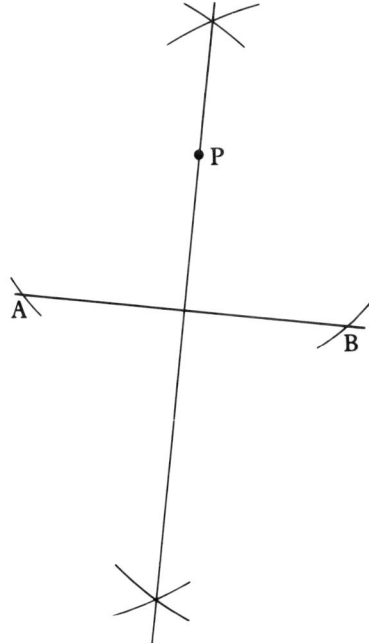

First draw arcs (centre P) to cut the line at A and B; then draw the perpendicular bisector of AB.

4

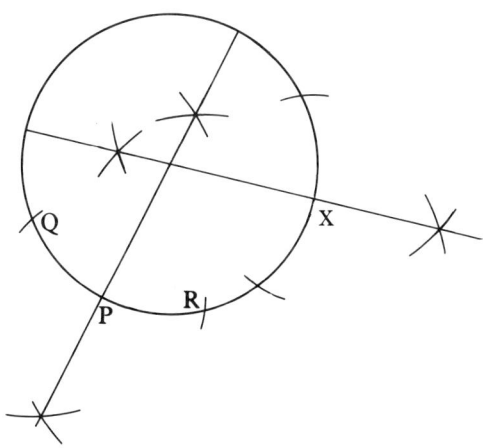

(a) First draw arcs to cut the circle at Q and R; then draw the perpendicular bisector of QR.
(b) To find the centre of the circle, repeat the procedure with a second point X, as shown. Alternatively construct the perpendicular bisector of the first diameter.

5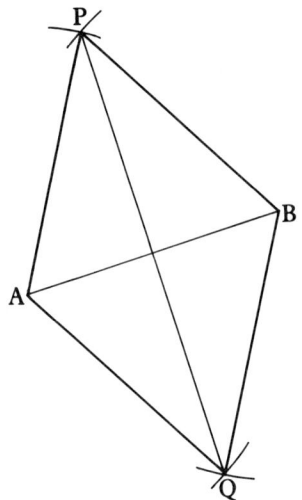

The lengths AP, AQ, BP and BQ are all the same because they were drawn using the same radius. APBQ is therefore a rhombus and the diagonals of a rhombus cross at right-angles.

8 Direct and inverse proportionality

This chapter opens with a brief review of direct proportionality and goes on to introduce inverse proportionality, and to contrast the two types of proportionality.

A Direct proportionality

A1 (a) £1·60 (b) £4·80 (c) £14·40
(d) £129·60

A2 (a) 51·1 (b) 14·7

A3 (a) 7·1 (b) 12·3

A4 (a) 5·3 (b) 22·5 (c) 8·0

B Inverse proportionality

B1 (a)
p	2	3	4	6	10	20	30	40
c	60	40	30	20	12	6	4	3

(b) The product pc is constant, 120.
(c) It is divided by 2.
(d) It is divided by 3.
(e) It is divided by 4.

B2 (a) 6 hours
(b)
s	6	10	20	30	40	50	60	80	100	120
t	40	24	12	8	6	4·8	4	3	2·4	2

(c) The product st is constant, 240.
(d) It is divided by 3.
(e)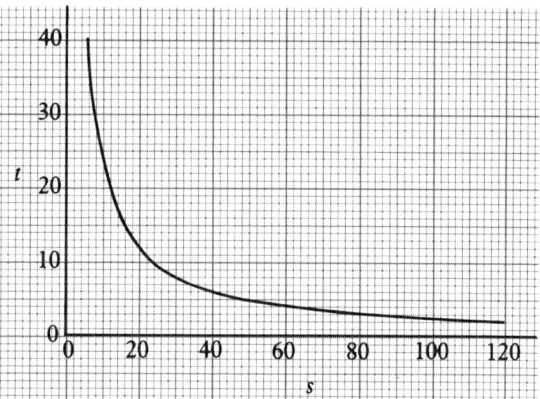

B3 (a) (i) 1·5 (ii) 12
(b) (i) 24 (ii) 13·3 (to 1 d.p.)

B4 55·7 cm (to 3 s.f.)

B5
Note	B	C	D	E	F	G
Length in cm (to 1 d.p.)	62·1	58·8	52·4	46·7	44·0	39·3

B6 52·5 cm

B7 (a) 375   (b) 300   (c) 162

B8 (a) 4·85   (b) 0·62

*B9 9·375 minutes

*B10 (a) (i) 20% increase   (ii) 20% increase
(b) (i) 16·7% decrease (to 3 s.f.)
(ii) 25% increase

9 Representing information

There are many kinds of problem whose solution is made considerably easier by finding a good way to represent the information given. Tables and diagrams of one kind or another can help us to 'take in' information and see relationships. This chapter gives some examples, but many other instances can be found throughout the course (e.g. the use of tree diagrams in combinatorial problems and probability).

A Networks

A1 Bottom row, third from left

A2 10 (see page 76 in pupil's book)

A3 (a)

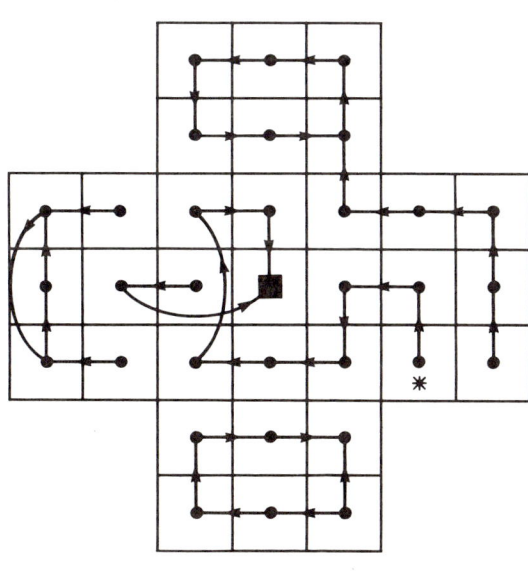

See the square marked * in the diagram.

(b) Three

A4 Very few pupils will be able to solve this puzzle at this stage. Two possible solutions are given on page 78 of the pupil's book and the remaining six are given below.

A5 Pupils will need to be encouraged to search systematically.
The other six solutions are
B D F A C E   or   E C A F D B
C E A B D F   or   F D B A E C
E C A B D F   or   F D B A C E
BDFAEC   or   CEAFDB

A6 (a)

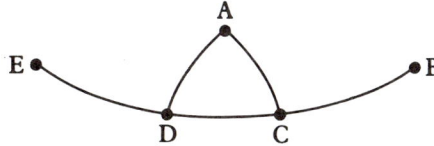

(b),(c) B C A D E   or   E D A C B
There just two related solutions.
(d) B and E
(e) It cannot be done. E, B and F can each only stand next to one person and there are only two ends to a line!

A7 (a)

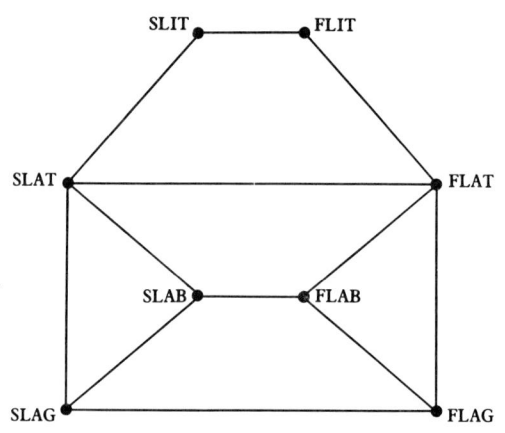

(b) FLAT FLAB FLAG SLAG SLAB SLAT SLIT FLIT
FLAT FLAG FLAB SLAB SLAG SLAT SLIT FLIT

These cover all possibilities but a pupil's list may start at any word in a list and continue either forwards or backwards.

A8

B Two-way tables

B1 A suggested approach is outlined on page 80 of the pupil's book.

	Like maths	Dislike maths	Total
Girls	48	11	59
Boys	29	28	57
Total	77	39	116

28 boys dislike maths.

B2 (a)

	Wear glasses	Do not wear glasses	Total
Girls	39	125	164
Boys	55	107	162
Total	94	232	326

(b) 162 boys

B3

	Metallic	Non-metallic	Total
Left-hand drive	82	27	109
Right-hand drive	185	288	473
Total	267	315	582

82 left-hand drive cars were painted with metallic paint.

B4 (a) Two-way tables must have 'either/or' labels; that is definite two-state categorisations.

In this case any pupil either does French, or does not. Similarly with German.

(b)

	French	No French	Total
German	146	125	271
No German	239	9	248
Total	385	134	519

(c) 9 pupils study neither of the languages.

B5

	Sugar	No sugar	Total
Milk	45%	30%	75%
No milk	20%	5%	25%
Total	65%	35%	100%

5% took neither sugar nor milk.

B6

	Men	Women	Total
Under 30	24%	37%	61%
30 or over	15%	24%	39%
Total	39%	61%	100%

61% of the members are women.

C Network tables

C1 (a) Because A is connected to B, C and F, but not to A, D and E.
(b) Because B is connected to A, C and D, but not to B, E and F.
(c)

	A	B	C	D	E	F
A	0	1	1	0	0	1
B	1	0	1	1	0	0
C	1	1	0	0	1	1
D	0	1	0	0	1	0
E	0	0	1	1	0	0
F	1	0	1	0	0	0

C2 (a)

	A	B	C	D	E
A	0	1	0	0	1
B	1	0	0	1	0
C	0	0	0	1	0
D	0	1	1	0	1
E	1	0	0	1	0

(b)

	A	B	C	D	E	F
A	0	1	0	1	1	1
B	1	0	1	1	0	0
C	0	1	0	1	0	0
D	1	1	1	0	1	0
E	1	0	0	1	0	1
F	1	0	0	0	1	0

(c)

	A	B	C	D	E	F
A	0	1	0	0	0	0
B	1	0	1	0	0	0
C	0	1	0	1	0	0
D	0	0	1	0	1	0
E	0	0	0	1	0	1
F	0	0	0	0	1	0

C3 (a)

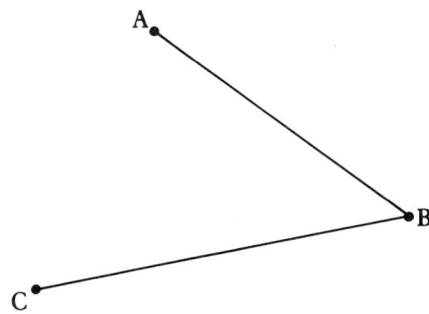

(b)

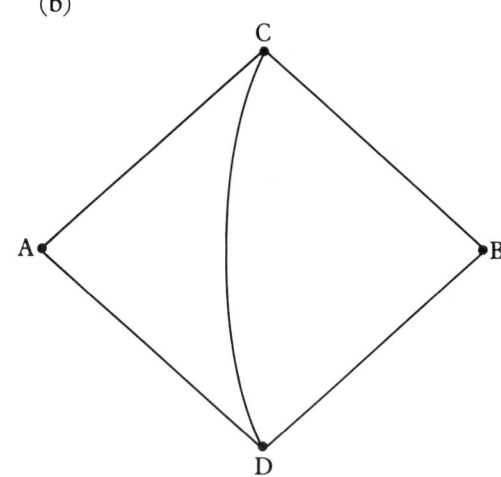

C4 In C1 (i) 8 (ii) 16
In C2 (a) (i) 5 (ii) 10
(b) (i) 9 (ii) 18
(c) (i) 5 (ii) 10
In C3 (a) (i) 2 (ii) 4
(b) (i) 5 (ii) 10

The total of all the numbers in the table is always twice the number of edges in the network. This is because each edge has two 'ends'.

C5 (a)

	A	B	C	D	E
A	0	3	1	0	2
B	3	0	1	0	0
C	1	1	0	3	0
D	0	0	3	0	1
E	2	0	0	1	0

(b) Yes, there are 11 edges and the total of all the numbers in the table is 22.

C6 (a) Because the total of all the numbers in the table is 20, the number of edges in the network is 10.

(b)

	A	B	C	D	E	F
A	0	1	1	1	1	1
B	1	0	1	1	1	1
C	1	1	0	1	1	1
D	1	1	1	0	1	1
E	1	1	1	1	0	1
F	1	1	1	1	1	0

The number of edges would be 15.

(c) The number of edges would be 21.
(d) (i) 45 (ii) 190 (iii) 4950

(e) There are n rows and n columns. In each row there are $(n–1)$ 1s and one 0. The total in each row is $(n–1)$. The total of all the rows is $n(n–1)$. The number of edges in the network is $\frac{n(n-1)}{2}$.

Algebra review (2)

1 (a) $x = 8$ (b) $x = {}^-25$
   (c) $x = 7$ (d) $x = 3$

2 (a) $5a + 8$ (b) $2b – 3$
   (c) $2c – 12$ (d) $2 + 9d$
   (e) $18e – 15$ (f) $^-5 – 8f$

3 (b) $2b(2 + 3c)$ (c) $2c(4c + 5)$
   (d) $3d(2 – 5d)$ (e) $4(3 – 2e^2)$
   (f) $2g(3f – 4g)$ (g) $2g(15 – 2g)$

4 (a) $4(a + b + c)$ (b) $2(ab + bc + ca)$
   (c) abc

5 (a) £$\frac{x}{a}$ (b) £$\frac{y}{b}$ (c) £$\frac{x+y}{a+b}$

6 (a) $r = \frac{s+t}{a}$ (b) $t = ar - s$
   (c) $m = a(g - n)$ (d) $x = \frac{tby}{a}$
   (e) $y = \frac{ax}{bt}$ (f) $x = \frac{h - ab}{b}$

10 Looking at data

This chapter introduces the median and its uses. The work is taken further in chapter 17.

A The median of a set of measurements

A1 (a) Number 6
   (b) Smallest 39 kg, median 52 kg, largest 63 kg, range 24 kg

A2 (a) Number 12
   (b) Smallest 3·1 m, median 5·2 m, largest 7·8 m, range 4·7 m

A3 (a) Numbers 8 and 9   (b) 168 cm

A4 (a) Numbers 7 and 8
   For n items, the numbers of the middle pair are $\frac{1}{2}n$ and $\frac{1}{2}n + 1$.
   (b) For n items, the number of the middle one is $\frac{1}{2}(n + 1)$.
   [Note: pupils will write these rules in their own way, not necessarily algebraically.]

A5
	Smallest	Median	Largest	Range
(a)	64	82	100	36
(b)	22	41	57	35
(c)	3·4	5·35	6·9	3·5

A6 Smallest 57 cm, median 73 cm, largest 88 cm, range 31 cm

B Stem-and-leaf tables

B1 73 marks

B2 (a) 4 | 5 8
        5 | 3 3 5 6
        6 | 0 1 4 4 7 8
        7 | 4 6
        8 | 3

(b) 60–69 is the modal group.
(c) 61 is the median mark.
(d) 38 is the range.

B3 (a)
1· | 6 8
2· | 3 5 5 6 7 8 8
3· | 0 0 3 5 6 9
4· | 0 1 1 2 3

(b) 3·0 kg

B4 (a) Paper 2 was harder than paper 1 because fewer pupils got high marks and more got low marks.
(b) 66 is the median mark for paper 1. 50 is the median mark for paper 2.
(c) 72 is the range for paper 1. 74 is the range for paper 2.

B5 (a)
Soil A
3 | 1 3 5 6 8 8 9
4 | 0 0 3 4 5 5 6 7 9 9
5 | 1 2 5 5 7 7 8
6 | 2 6 9
7 | 3

Soil B
3 | 7 8
4 | 2 5 8 9
5 | 0 2 4 4 6
6 | 1 1 4 5 5 7 8 9
7 | 0 0 1 1 2 4

(b)
	Shortest	Median	Longest	Range
Soil A	31 mm	46·5 mm	73 mm	42 mm
Soil B	37 mm	61 mm	74 mm	37 mm

(c) As a group the worms in soil B are longer than the worms in soil A. The worms in soil A are more widely spread out in length.

C Averages : median and mean

Note: This section will require a good deal of discussion.

C1 (a) £330 is the median.
(b) £547 is the mean.
(c) The median gives a better idea because, apart from nine very high earners, the earnings are all in the range £250–£390.
(d) The median   (e) The mean
(f) 9 employees

C2 (a) 34·5 hours is the median.
(b) 28·2 hours is the mean.
(c) The median gives a better idea because, apart from six batteries, the lifetimes are all in the range 29–42 hours.

If all you have is ... (page 91)

1 $ad = bd$ so $a = b$

2 Draw lines parallel to the arms of the angle using the strip.

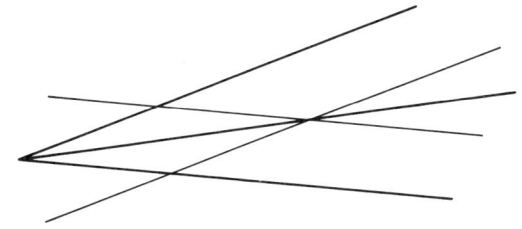

3 Twist the strip until its parallel edges are at P and Q, then draw parallel lines.
Then twist it in the opposite direction and draw a second pair of parallel lines.

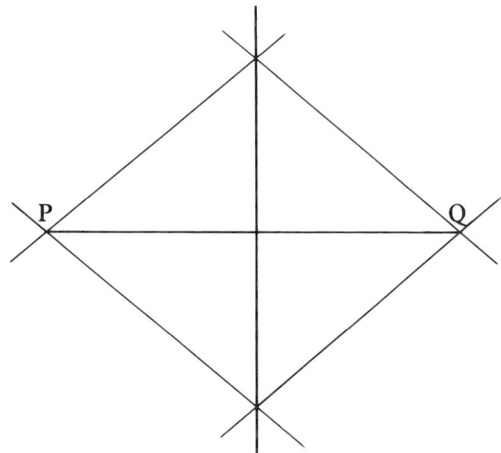

4 Draw parallel lines through the ends of the line, P and Q, as in 3.
Now draw a third line parallel to the first two. Extend PQ to meet the third line.

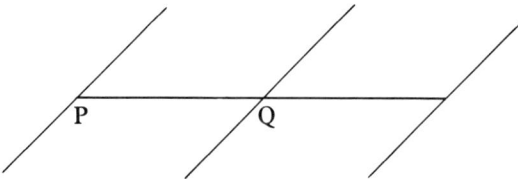

5 Draw any three equally spaced parallel lines with the middle one through P and the right-hand one cutting the original line at Q.
Now draw a pair of parallel lines through P and Q as in 3.
A perpendicular through P can then be drawn as shown.

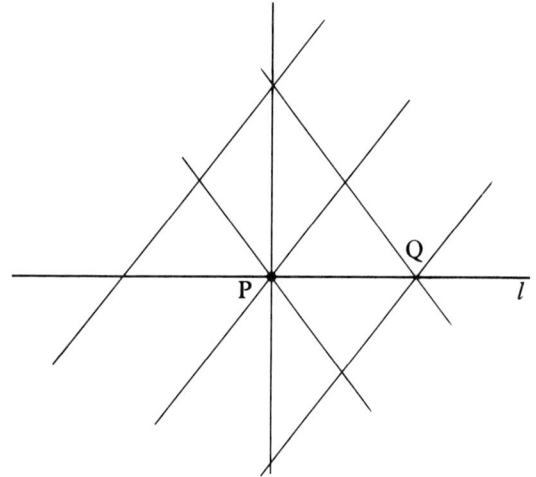

6 The required square will be drawn on the diagonal of the original square.
The order in which the lines were drawn is given.

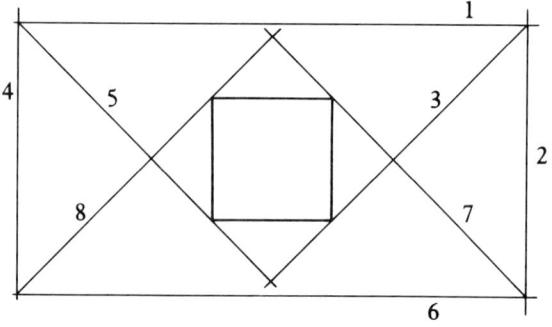

7 Construct perpendiculars at the ends P and Q as in 5.
Draw lines parallel to the perpendiculars using the strip. Extend PQ to meet these lines at X and Y.
Now construct the perpendicular of XY as in 3.

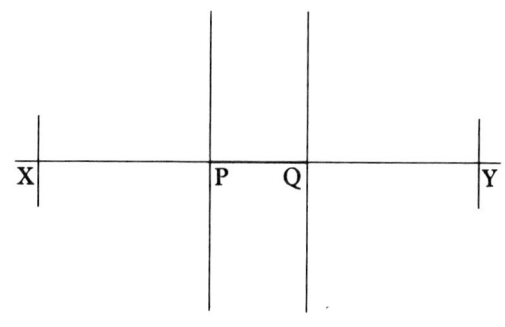

11 Percentage (2)

The 'multiplier' approach to percentage increase and decrease, introduced in *Book Y1*, comes into its own here in the sections dealing with successive percentage changes, such as compound interest.

A **Percentages of percentages**

A1 21%

A2 16%

A3 (a)

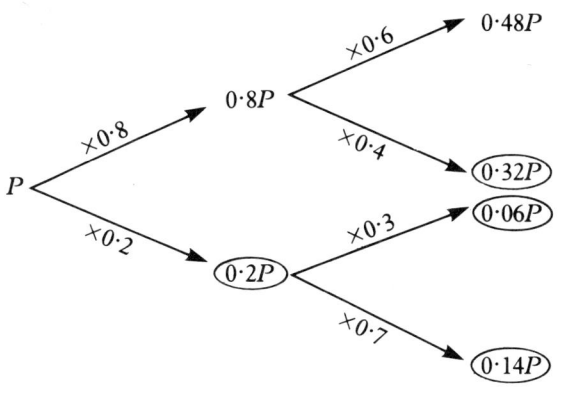

(b) (i) 32% (ii) 6% (iii) 14%
(c) 48 + 32 + 6 + 14 = 100

A4 (a)

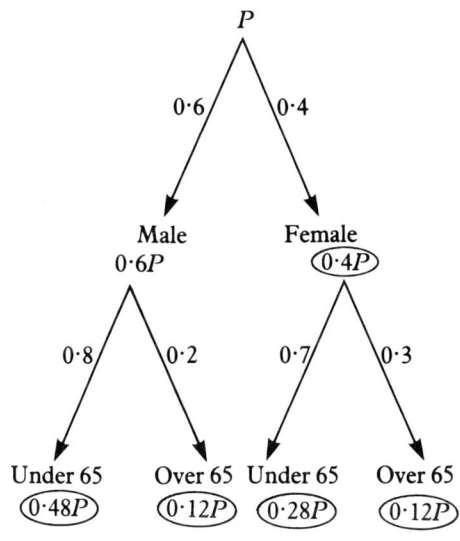

(b) Male under 65, 48%;
male over 65, 12%
Female under 65, 28%;
female over 65, 12%
(c) 76%

A5 (a)

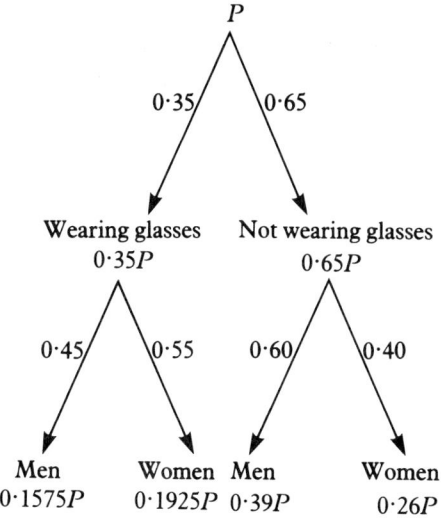

(b) Men wearing glasses, 15·75%;
women wearing glasses, 19·25%;
men not wearing glasses, 39%;
women not wearing glasses, 26%

A6 44·08%

B Percentage increases and decreases

B1 (a) 1·25 (b) 1·13 (c) 1·20
(d) 1·08 (e) 1·165

B2 (a) 82% (b) 82% (c) 21·5% (d) 44%

B3 (a) 0·86 (b) 0·93 (c) 0·78 (d) 0·755
(e) 0·965

B4 (a) 44% (b) 23·56% (c) 20·79%

B5 (a) 1·15 (b) 0·92 (c) 5·8% increase

B6 5% increase

B7 2·5% decrease

The remaining parts of this chapter are concerned with compound interest and/or flow charts. These ideas will require a good deal of discussion.

B8 (a) £53 (b) £56·18 (c) £59·55
(d) £63·12 (e) £66·91

B9

Number of years	Amount
0	£240
1	£252
2	£264·60
3	£277·83
4	£291·72
5	£306·31
6	£321·62
7	£337·70
8	£354·59
9	£372·32
10	£390·93

B10

Number of years	Amount
0	£ 40
1	£ 43·60
2	£ 47·52
3	£ 51·80
4	£ 56·46
5	£ 61·54
6	£ 67·08
7	£ 73·12
8	£ 79·70
9	£ 86·88
10	£ 94·69
11	£103·22

B11 (a) Value after 7 years: £1443 (to nearest pound)

(b) Time taken (in whole years): 14 years

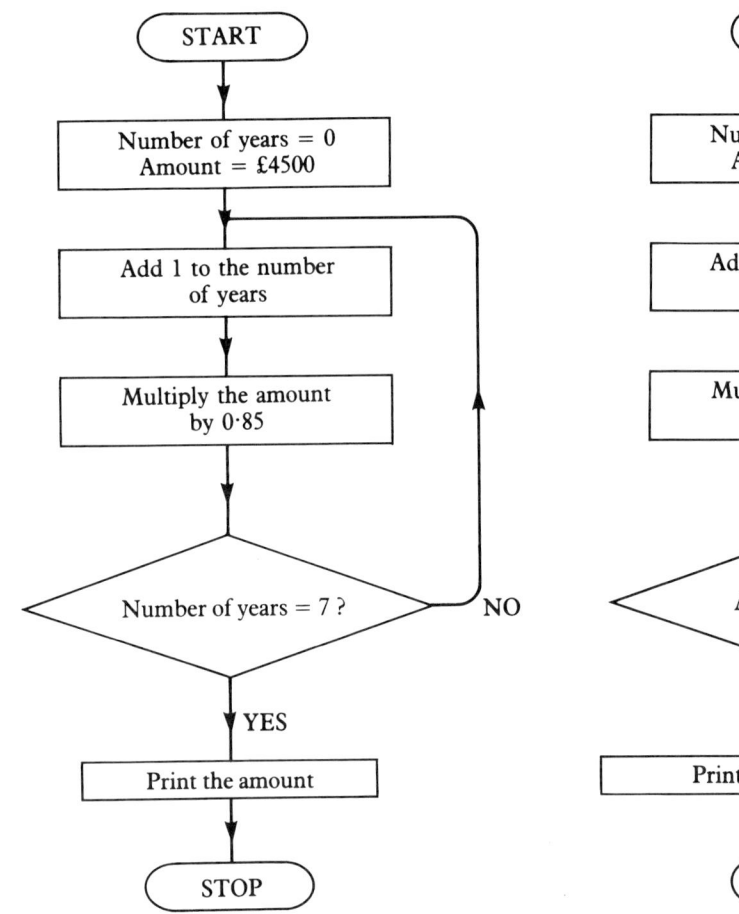

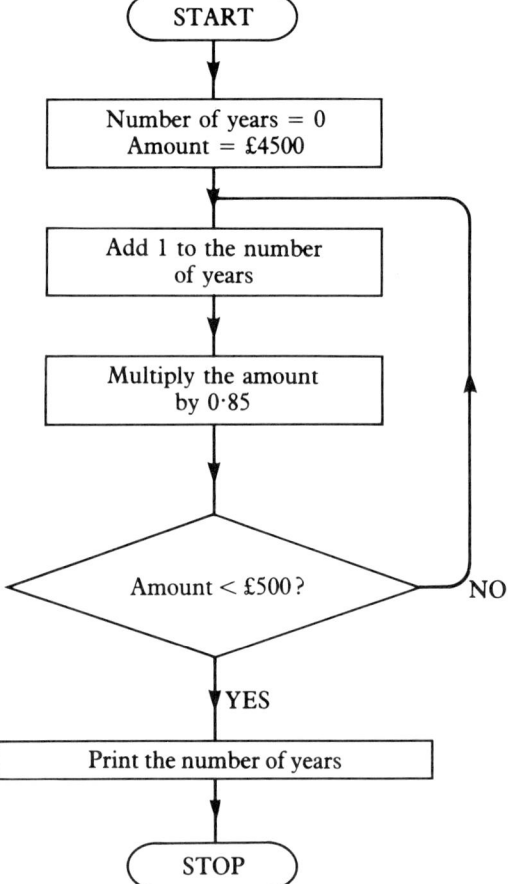

12 Investigations (2)

These investigations, based on the Morse code, are intended as a class activity. Although pupils may work alone on parts of the investigation, it is intended that there should be discussion of methods and results as the work proceeds.

A The Morse code

A1 DO
NOT
DECODE
THIS
MESSAGE

A2 There are only 30 possible codes without extending to five symbols. The most efficient codings of the Russian alphabet will therefore have just one letter with a five-symbol code.

A3 He considered E and T to be the most commonly used letters.

A4 (a) 4   (b) 8   (c) 16

A5 The number of extra letters doubles each time because each of the possibilities for the previous stage can be extended with either a dash or a dot; for example, the 4 possible two-symbol codes

```
• •          — •
— —          • —
```

give rise to the following 8 three-symbol codes

```
• • •        — • •
• — •        — • —
• — •        — — •
• • —        — — —
```

B How many sequences?

B1 (a) 1   (b) 2   (c) 3   (d) 4   (e) 5

B2

Number of dashes	0	1	2	3	4	5	6	7
Number of different sequences with 1 dot	1	2	3	4	5	6	7	8

B3 (a) 1   (b) 3   (c) 6   (d) 10

B4

Number of dashes

Number of dots	0	1	2	3	4	5
1	1	2	3	4	5	6
2	1	3	6	10	15	21
3	1	4	10	20	35	56
4	1	5	15	35	70	126
5	1	6	21	56	126	252

Lots of number patterns are present in the table, which is essentially a form of Pascal's triangle.
Each number is the sum of the number above it and the number on the left.
[Some pupils might be asked to explain why this should be so.]

B5

Number of dashes

Number of dots	0	1	2	3	4	5
0	—	1	1	1 (a)	1	1 (b)
1	1	2	3	4	5	6
2	1	3	6	10	15	21
3	1	4	10	20	35	56
4	1	5	15	35	70	126
5	1	6	21	56	126	252

B6 1 307 504

The sequences with 15 dots and 9 dashes can be thought of as arising

either by having a dot in front of each of the possible sequences with 14 dots and 9 dashes

or by having a dash in front of each of the possible sequences with 15 dots and 8 dashes.

C 'Length' of a sequence

C1

Length of sequence	1	2	3	4	5
Number of different sequences	1	2	3	5	8
6	7	8	9	10	...
13	21	34	55	89	...

Each term (from the third term onwards) is the sum of the previous two terms.

This pattern arises because all the sequences of length 4, say, can be constructed either by adding a dash on the end of each sequence of length 2, or by adding a dot on the end of each sequence of length 3. This pattern continues indefinitely.

C2

Length of sequence	1	2	3	4	5
Number of different sequences	1	1	2	3	4
6	7	8	9	10	...
6	9	13	19	28	...

In this sequence each term (from the fourth term onwards) is the sum of the previous term and the term three places back.

This pattern arises because all the sequences of length 4, say, can be constructed either by adding a dash on the end of each sequence of length 1, or by adding a dot on the end of each sequence of length 3.

Algebra review (3)

1 (a) 3 hours (b) $\frac{a}{u}$ (c) $\frac{a}{u} + \frac{a}{v}$

   (d) (i) $\frac{a}{x}$ m.p.h. (ii) $\frac{a}{y}$ m.p.h.

   (iii) $\frac{2a}{x+y}$ m.p.h.

2 (a) $a = 180 - 7x$
   $b = 180 - 4x$
   (b) $(180 - 7x) + (180 - 4x) + x = 180$
   $x = 18$

3 (a) $x^2 + 6x + 9$ (b) $x^2 - 8x + 16$
   (c) $4x^2 + 4x + 1$ (d) $9x^2 - 12x + 4$
   (e) $25x^2 + 40x + 16$ (f) $4 - 12x + 9x^2$

4 (a) $(2\frac{1}{2})^2 = 6\frac{1}{4}$
   $(5\frac{1}{2})^2 = 30\frac{1}{4}$
   $(7\frac{1}{2})^2 = 56\frac{1}{4}$
   (b) To work out $(n + \frac{1}{2})^2$, do $n(n + 1) + \frac{1}{4}$
   (c) $(n + \frac{1}{2})^2 = (n + \frac{1}{2})(n + \frac{1}{2}) = n^2 + n + \frac{1}{4}$
   $n(n + 1) + \frac{1}{4} = n^2 + n + \frac{1}{4}$
   So the rule will be true for all values of n.

13 Right-angled triangles

Work on Pythagoras' rule is extended to three-dimensional problems in this chapter, and there is a brief review of trigonometry applied to two-dimensional problems.

A Pythagoras' rule

A1 (a) 6·40 cm (b) 15 cm
(c) 9·90 cm (d) 17·09 cm
(all except (b) to 2 d.p.)

A2 14·42 cm (to 2 d.p.)

A3 14·14 cm (to 2 d.p.)

A4 (a) 9·54 cm (b) 7·55 cm
(c) 13·93 cm (d) 10·72 cm
(e) 18·44 cm (all to 2 d.p.)

A5 (a) 7·21 (b) 4·58
(c) 3·87 (d) 12·29 (all to 2 d.p.)

A6 (a) 8·66 cm (b) 43·3 cm² (both to 3 s.f.)

A7

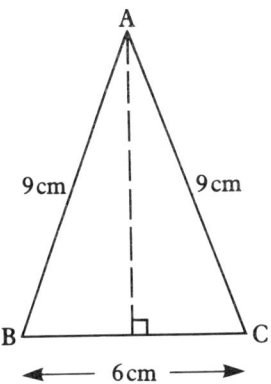

(a) 8·49 cm (b) 25·5 cm² (both to 3 s.f.)

A8 15·2 cm (to 3 s.f.)

A9

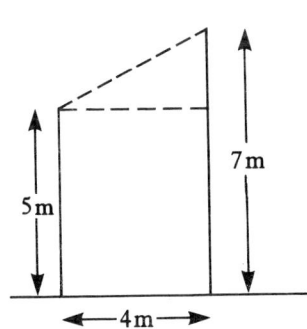

4·47 m (to 2 d.p.)

A10 10·95 cm (to 2 d.p.)

A11 8·66 cm (to 2 d.p.)

B The distance between two points whose coordinates are given

B1

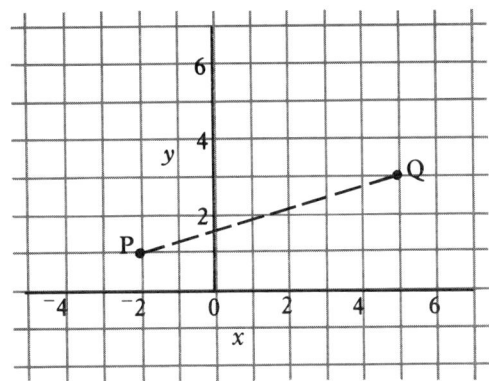

7·28 (to 2 d.p.)

B2 5·39 (to 2 d.p.)

B3 (a) 6·32 (b) 5 (c) 7·28
(d) 9·22 (all except (b) to 2 d.p.)

B4 (a) Inside (b) Outside (c) On
(d) Inside (e) Inside

B5 6·32 (to 2 d.p.), 5, 6·71 (to 2 d.p.)

B6 A and C are furthest apart.
B and C are closest together.

B7 13·04 km (to 2 d.p.)

C Proving Pythagoras' rule

C1 $(a + b)^2 = a^2 + b^2 + 2ab$ (from first square)
$(a + b)^2 = c^2 + 2ab$ (from second square)
So $a^2 + b^2 = c^2$.

Pupils will often express this argument informally in their own terms. This should be encouraged. It is vital not to give the impression that there is only one valid form of the explanation!

D Acute angles and obtuse angles in triangles

D1 (a) Obtuse (b) P acute, R acute

D2 (a) X acute, Y acute, Z acute
(b) X acute, Y acute, Z acute

49

E A nomogram for Pythagoras' rule

E1 (a) 9·7 (b) 7·2 (c) 9·1

E2 Using the nomogram with $a = 4$ and $b = 7$, XZ would be 8·1 if the angle at Y were a right-angle.
Since XZ is in fact 9, the angle at Y must be obtuse.

F Three-dimensional problems

F1 (a) 14·14 cm (b) 17·32 cm (both to 2 d.p.)

F2 10·25 cm (to 2 d.p.)

F3

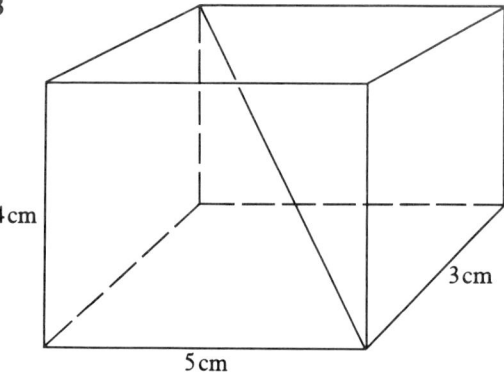

7·07 cm (to 2 d.p.)

F4 (a) The angle at Q
(b) PR = 14·14 m,
PC = 7·07 m (both to 2 d.p.)
(c) The angle at C (d) 13·93 m (to 2 d.p.)

F5 5·57 m (to 2 d.p.)

F6 (a) 8·06 m (b) 9·49 m
(c) 8·60 m (d) 34·4 m² (all to 3 s.f.)

F7 (a) $a = 5·66$ cm, $s = 8·25$ cm
(both to 2 d.p.)
(b) $b = 7·21$ cm, $s = 8·25$ cm
(both to 2 d.p.)
(c) 28·8 cm² (to 3 s.f.)

F8
8·66 cm (to 2 d.p.)

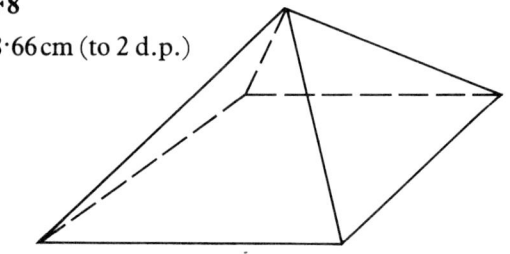

G Trigonometry

G1 (a) 3·1 cm (b) 4·2 cm (c) 7·8 cm
(d) 66·4° (e) 61·7° (f) 15·9°
(g) 8·9 cm

All the remaining answers are given to 3 s.f.
Some variation can be expected in pupils' answers where they are using rounded versions in subsequent work.

G2 $a = 3·61$ cm, $b = 7·75$ cm,
$c = 4·38$ cm, $d = 10·5$ cm

G3 (a) 4·53 cm (b) 15·9 cm²

G4

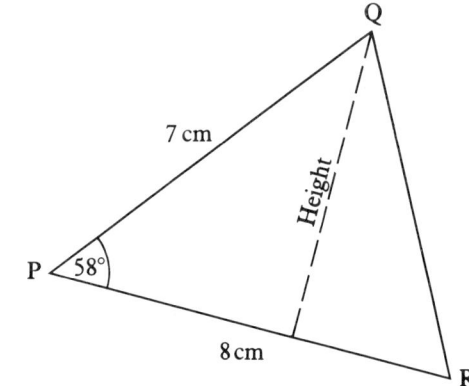

(a) 5·94 cm (b) 23·7 cm²

G5

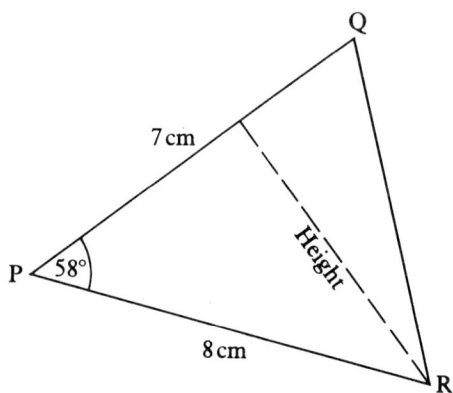

(a) 6·78 cm (b) 23·7 cm² (c) No

G6

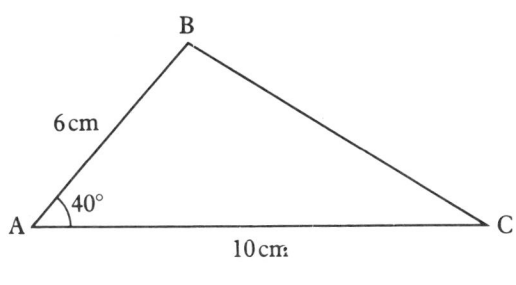

19·3 cm²

G7 (a) 7·62 km (b) 5·33 km
(c) 3·97 km (d) 15·9 km
(e) (i) 11·6 km (ii) 21·2 km
(f) 24·2 km (g) 061·4°

G8 (a) 3·66 km (b) 9·52 km
(c) 6·28 km (d) 2·04 km
(e) (i) 9·93 km (ii) 11·6 km
(f) 15·2 km (g) 049·4°

G9 (a) 15·3 km (b) 12·9 km
(c) 3·42 km south (d) 9·40 km
(e) (i) 11·9 km (ii) 22·3 km
(f) 25·3 km (g) 061·9°

Review 2

8 Direct and inverse proportionality

8.1 (a) 23·7 g (b) 21·1 amps (both to 3 s.f.)

8.2 (a) 2·24 kg/m³ (b) 8·4 m³

8.3 32·1 cm (to 3 s.f.)

9 Representing information

9.1 (a) Yes, 2 ways; M S K H J G and reversal
(b) No, because Mary and Gary have only one friend each.
(c) Yes, 4 ways; H K J G M S and reversal, H K S M G J and reversal
(d) No, because Hitesh now has only one friend.
(e) Yes, 2 ways; H S M G J K clockwise and anticlockwise

9.2 6%

9.3 (a) Vertex A lies on edges p, q, r and u, but not on s and t.

(b)

	p	q	r	s	t	u
A	1	1	1	0	0	1
B	1	0	0	0	0	0
C	0	1	0	1	1	0
D	0	0	1	1	0	0
E	0	0	0	0	1	1

(c) Every edge has two ends.

10 Looking at data

10.1 (a) 15 kg (b) 51 kg (c) 50 kg

10.2 (a) **Boys**
4 | 1 4 4 7 7 8
5 | 0 3 3 3 3 3 3 4 5 8 9
6 | 0 0 2 6 9
7 | 0 0 3

Girls
3 | 5 9
4 | 0 0 2 7 7 8 8 8 9 9
5 | 0 0 2 4 4 4 4 4 5 7 8
6 | 0 2 3 4 8
7 | 0

(b)

	Smallest	Median	Largest	Range
Boys	41 kg	53 kg	73 kg	32 kg
Girls	35 kg	53 kg	70 kg	35 kg

11 Percentage (2)

11.1 36%

11.2 (a) 15·75% (b) 32·25% (c) 52%

11.3 (a) 64·56% increase
(b) 29·48% decrease
(c) 17·92% decrease

11.4

Date	Outstanding amount
1st Sept	£800·00
1st Oct	£716·00
1st Nov	£630·32
1st Dec	£542·93
1st Jan	£453·78
1st Feb	£362·86
1st Mar	£270·12
1st Apr	£175·52
1st May	£ 79·03
1st June	⁻£ 19·39

Discussion would be needed regarding the significance of the negative outstanding amount and the likely methods of actually settling the debt.

13 Right-angled triangles

13.1 7·48 cm (to 3 s.f.)

13.2 7·81 (to 3 s.f.)

13.3 (a) 6·88 cm (b) 33·7 cm² (both to 3 s.f.)

13.4 (a) The angle at B (b) Greater than 90°

13.5

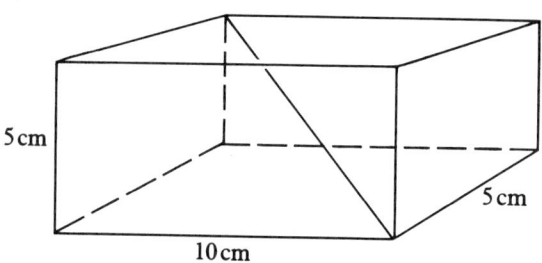

12·2 cm (to 3 s.f.)

13.6 (a) 1·91 m (b) 1·66 m (c) 2·11 m (all to 3 s.f.)

14 Volume

This chapter deals mainly with the volumes of prisms, including the cylinder.

A Cuboids and prisms

A1 164·3 cm³

A2 (a) 42·9 m³ (b) 42 900 litres

A3 Pupil's own estimate, checked by discussion

A4 0·5 m

A5 (a) 0·50 m (b) 0·078 m (both to 2 s.f.)

A6 3·6 cm

A7 (a) 63 cm³ (b) 56 cm³ (c) 40 cm³

A8 (a) About 16 cm² (b) About 56 cm³

A9 (a) 13 cm² (b) 39 cm³

A10 (a) (i) 10 cm² (ii) 70 cm³
(b) (i) 14 m² (ii) 77 m³

A11 13·5 cm³

A12 52 cm²

A13 0·02 cm

A14 (a) 6·93 cm (b) 27·7 cm² (c) 277 cm³ (d) 721 g (all to 3 s.f.)

B Cylinders

B1 (a) 50·3 cm² (b) 377 cm³ (both to 3 s.f.)

B2 (a) 401 cm³ (to 3 s.f.)
(b) 360 g (to 3 s.f. with no rounding)

B3 (a) Using 3 as an approximation for π,
(i) 6 litres (ii) 12 litres
(iii) 1·5 litres
(b) (i) 6·28 litres (ii) 12·6 litres
(iii) 1·57 litres (all to 3 s.f.)

B4 About 500 litres

B5 The volume of A is 4 times as much as the volume of B.

C Pyramids and cones

C1

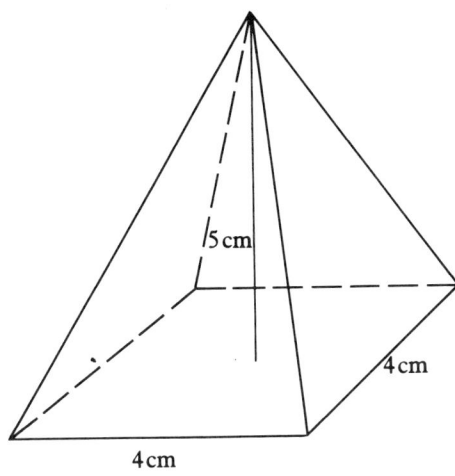

26·7 cm³ (to 3 s.f.)

C2 (a) 36 cm³ (b) 36 cm³

C3 314 cm³ (to 3 s.f.)

C4 $h = \dfrac{3V}{\pi r^2}$

C5 4·4

C6 (a) Few pupils will guess 20%.
(b) 21·6%

---

15 Problems in planning

Problems like those in this chapter arise frequently in organisations, such as companies, which have to plan and timetable their activities. (Of course in practice the problems are on a far larger scale.) The chapter also provides further illustrations of the value of diagrams to represent complex information.

There is often a variety of solutions to these problems. Time must be given to a full and detailed discussion of the merits or otherwise of the solutions found.

A Holidays

A1 The chief buyer and his secretary are both away in week 6.
Both secretaries are away in week 5.
There are only 3 people present in week 2.

A2 Here is one possible solution:

Week no.	1	2	3	4	5	6	7	8
Store manager		■	■					
Store manager's secretary						■	■	
Chief cashier				■	■			
Chief buyer	■	■						
Chief buyer's secretary							■	■
Transport supervisor				■	■			

A3 (a) Yes, it is possible. The store manager does not have to change her weeks. Here is one possible solution.

Week no.	1	2	3	4	5	6	7	8
Store manager		■	■					
Store manager's secretary				■	■			
Chief cashier						■	■	
Chief buyer				■	■			
Chief buyer's secretary	■	■						
Transport supervisor						■	■	

(b) It can be done in weeks 2 to 7 without changing the store manager's weeks.

It can be done in the first 6 weeks only if the store manager changes her weeks. For example:

Week no.	1	2	3	4	5	6	7	8
Store manager	■	■						
Store manager's secretary			■	■				
Chief cashier					■	■		
Chief buyer			■	■				
Chief buyer's secretary	■	■						
Transport supervisor					■	■		

A4 Here is one possible solution.

Week no.	1	2	3	4	5	6	7	8
Manager					▓	▓		
Caretaker		▓	▓	▓				
Clerical staff 1	▓	▓						
Clerical staff 2			▓	▓				
Instructor 1					▓	▓		
Instructor 2							▓	▓

A5 It can be done in weeks 2 to 8 without changing the caretaker's weeks. For example:

Week no.	1	2	3	4	5	6	7	8
Manager					▓	▓		
Caretaker		▓	▓	▓				
Clerical staff 1		▓	▓					
Clerical staff 2							▓	▓
Instructor 1					▓	▓		
Instructor 2							▓	▓

It can be done in weeks 1 to 7 only if the caretaker moves his holidays.

B Work

B1 (a) (i) 1st May (ii) 1st February
  (b) (i) A, 1st March 1992
      B, 1st January 1992
      C, 1st October 1991
      D, 1st July 1992
      E, 1st February 1993
      F, 1st December 1992
    (ii) Block C
    (iii) 27 months

B2 $7\frac{1}{2}$ hours

B3 (a) $4\frac{3}{4}$ hours
  (b) It will take $\frac{1}{4}$ hour longer.
  (c) No effect (d) No effect

B4 Yes, $1\frac{1}{2}$ hours later

B5 $3\frac{3}{4}$ hours from the start

B6 Repair ceilings

B7

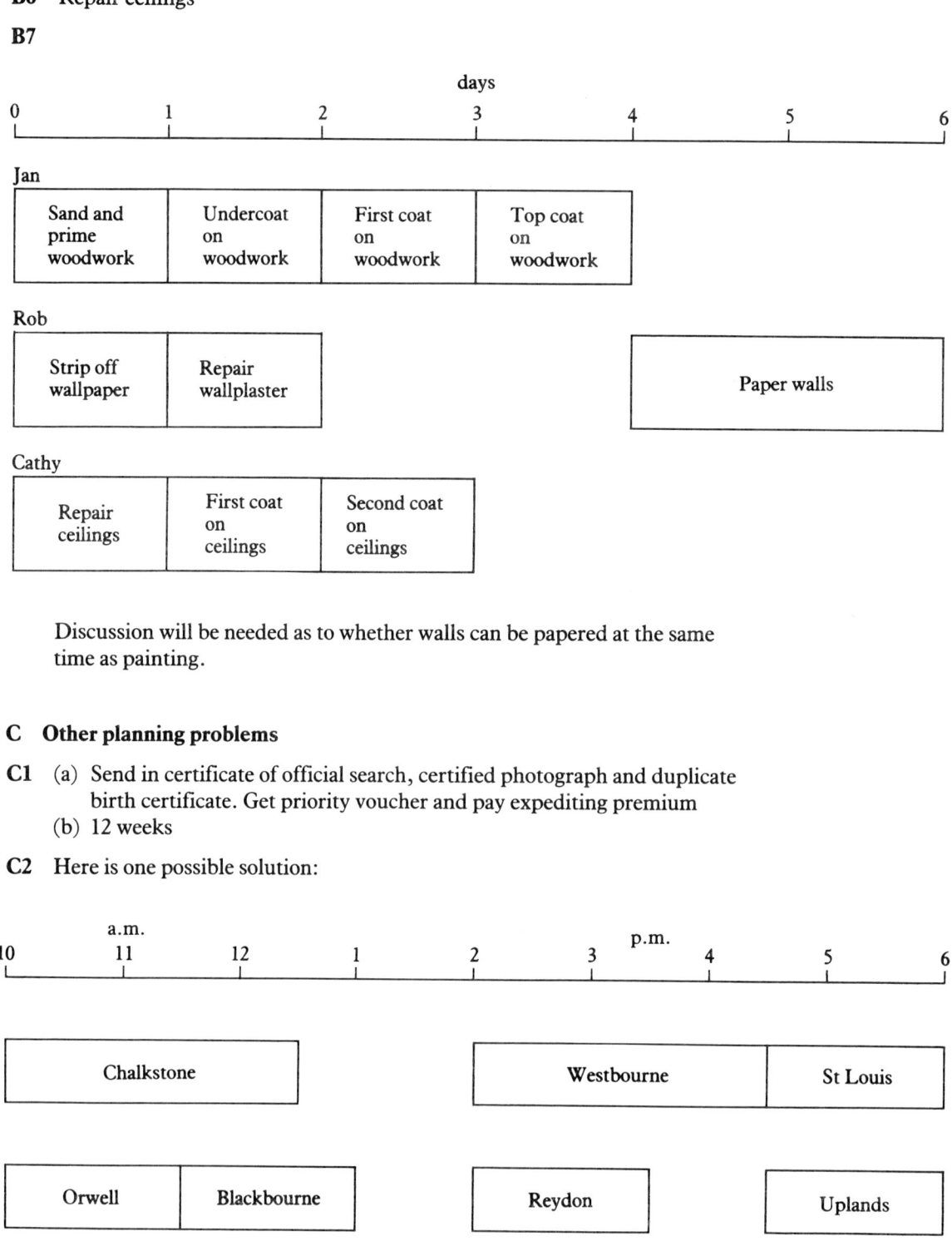

Discussion will be needed as to whether walls can be papered at the same time as painting.

C Other planning problems

C1 (a) Send in certificate of official search, certified photograph and duplicate birth certificate. Get priority voucher and pay expediting premium
 (b) 12 weeks

C2 Here is one possible solution:

16 Linear equations

Sections A and B of this chapter are about combining pairs of linear equations to derive further information from them. (In section A the 'equations' are presented non-algebraically so as to focus attention on the process of thinking, rather than on algebraic technique.) Sections C, D and E deal with simple cases of finding the common solution of a pair of equations by the 'elimination' method.

A Some puzzles

A1 (a) £1·38 (b) £1·00 (c) 38p
(d) 19p (e) 12p (f) 7p

A2 (a) $8\frac{1}{2}$g (b) 49g (c) 7g
(d) $1\frac{1}{2}$g (e) $5\frac{1}{2}$g

A3 The missing amounts are
760p
284p
568p
238p
330p

A4 (a) The missing amounts are
£10
£22
£32
£ 4
(b) £0·40   (c) £1
(d) For Ling $(45 \times 0.4) + 3 = 21$ ✓
For Instone $(25 \times 0.4) + 1 = 11$ ✓

A5 (a) Woodville should be £4500.
(b) £1   (c) £0·50

B Using letters

B1 (a) $2a + 6b = 36$ (b) $5a + 8b = 62$
(c) $3a + 2b = 26$

B2 (a) $6p + 15q = 201$ (b) $12p + 28q = 332$
(c) $5p + 12q = 150$ (d) $p + 2q = 16$

B3 (a) True (b) True
(c) False, $30f + 15g = 240$
(d) False, $3f + 2g = 29$
(e) False, $45f + 25g = 385$

B4 (a) $4a + 6b = 32$ (b) $2b = 4$ (c) $b = 2$
(d) $a = 5$
(e) $2a + 3b = (2 \times 5) + (3 \times 2) = 16$ ✓

B5 (a) $2x + 2y = 70$
$3x + y = 75$
(b) $x + y = 35$ (c) $2x = 40$
(d) $x = 20$ (e) $y = 15$
(f) 80p (g) 60p

B6 (a) $7a + 3b = 311$
$4a + b = 162$
(b) $12a + 3b = 486$
(c) $5a = 175$, so $a = 35$
(d) $b = 22$

C Common solutions of two equations

C1 $a + 3b = 5 + (3 \times 4) = 17$ ✓
$4a + 3b = (4 \times 5) + (3 \times 4) = 32$ ✓

C2 $a = 2$, $b = 15$

C3 $a = 3\frac{1}{2}$, $b = 3$

C4 $a = 3$, $b = 4$

C5 (a) (i) $2p + 4q = 54$ (ii) $3p + 6q = 81$
(iii) $4p + 8q = 108$
(iv) $5p + 10q = 135$
(b) part (ii), $q = 10$, $p = 7$

C6 (a) $f = 1$, $g = 4$
(b) $s = 2$, $r = 5$
(c) $b = 3$, $a = 8$

C7 (a) $b = 1$, $a = 5$
(b) $h = 4$, $k = 1$
(c) $v = 3$, $u = 3$

57

D Elimination by adding equations

D1 (a) $2a + 4b = 22$
(b) No

D2 (a) $a = 3$, $b = 2$ (b) $a = 6$, $b = 4$
(c) $p = 7$, $q = 1$

D3 $p = 5$, $q = 7$

D4 (a) $s = 4$, $t = 1$ (b) $r = 2$, $s = 1$
(c) $h = 6$, $k = 3$

D5 (a) $x = 4$, $y = 5$ (b) $x = 6$, $y = 5$
(c) $x = 1$, $y = 7$

E Intersecting lines

E1 $(4, {}^-3)$

E2 $(5, 1)$

E3 (a) $({}^-2, 6)$ (b) $(7, 1)$

E4 $({}^-12, 20)$

E5 (a) $(4, {}^-3)$ (b) $({}^-3, 7)$

E6 $(20, 12)$, $({}^-4, 24)$, $(8, {}^-12)$

17 Distributions

This chapter reverses the usual order of presenting a cumulative frequency graph as a construct out of an ordinary frequency table. (Such cumulative frequency graphs are largely guesswork between known points.) The 'box plot', introduced in section A, is a convenient way of representing the extremes, the median and the quartiles of a distribution.

A Percentiles

A1 (a) 50 (b) 80 (c) 270
(d) About 2550 hours (e) About 370 hours

A2 (a) About 1730 hours (b) About 1980 hours
(c) 3000 hours (d) 3350 hours

A3 (a) 16th (b) 86th (both to 2 s.f.)

A4 (a) 2600 hours (b) 2820 hours

A5 (a) 200 hours (b) 1400 hours (c) 1900 hours
(d) 2400 hours (e) 3200 hours
(f)

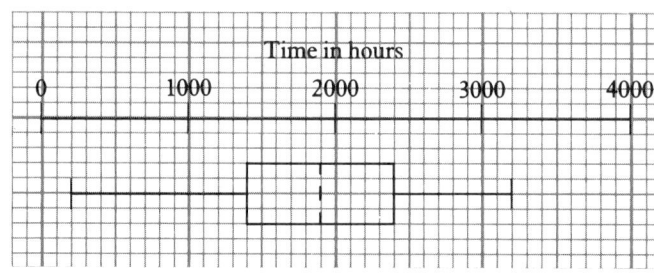

A6 (a)

	Brand A	Brand B
Minimum	2	1
Maximum	10	12
Median	6	7
Lower quartile	4	5
Upper quartile	7	8·6

(b)

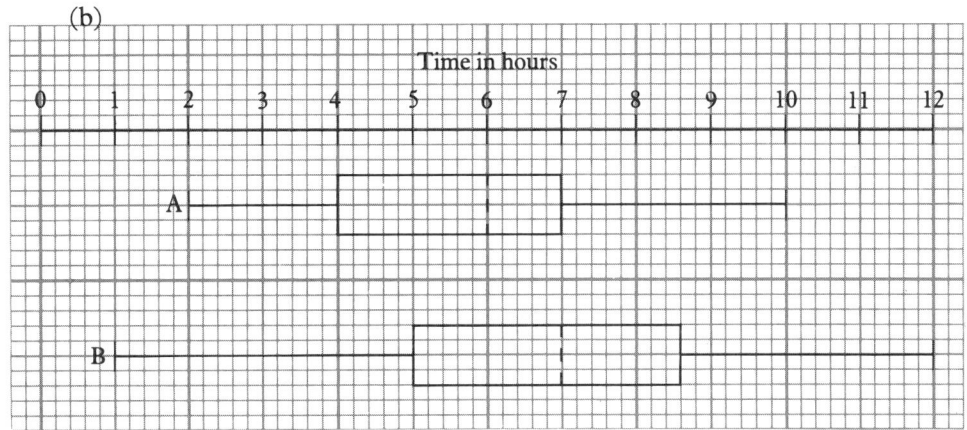

(c) Brand B appears to be better.

B Cumulative frequency

B1 (a) 90 (b) 134 (c) 182

B2 (a) 200 (b) 75 (c) 125

B3 (a) 20% (b) About 95%

B4 (a) Lower quartile 47 g;   median 59 g;   upper quartile 72 g

(b)

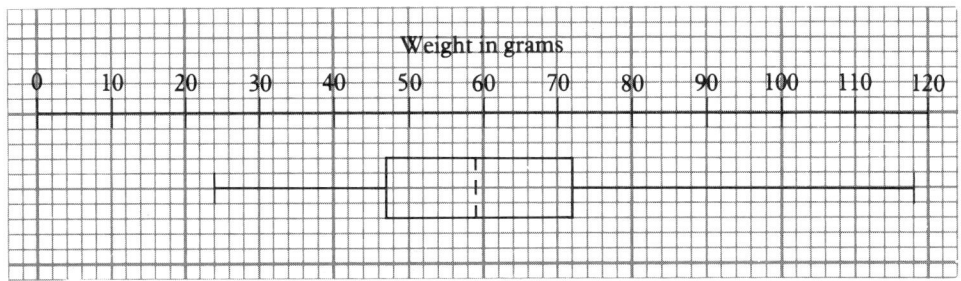

B5 Lower quartile 70 cm;   median 77 cm;   upper quartile 82 cm

B6 (a) (i) Half of the population of town A are below the age of 35 years.
　　　(ii) Half of the population of town B are below the age of 56 years.
　　　(iii) 4% of the population of town A are 80 or over.
　　　(iv) 11% of the population of town B are 80 or over.
　(b) Town A is likely to be the new town and town B the seaside town.
　(c) Lower quartile 16 years; upper quartile 60 years.
　(d) Lower quartile 38 years; upper quartile 70 years.
　(e) The 50–60 age-group

C The inter-quartile range

C1　25 grams

C2　(a)

	A	B
Lower quartile	11 cm	13 cm
Median	15 cm	21 cm
Upper quartile	20 cm	24 cm

　(b)

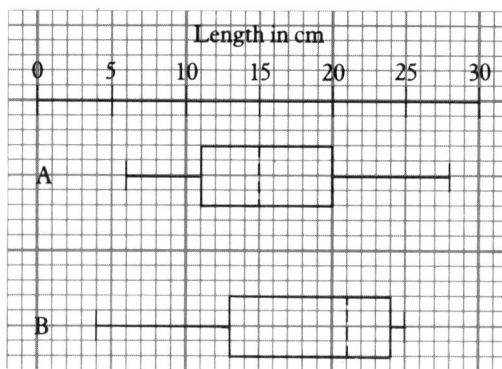

　(c) A, 9 cm; B, 11 cm
　(d) In population B the lengths are more widely spread out on the whole.

D Frequency and cumulative frequency

D1

Lifetime in hours	Frequency (number of bulbs)
0–1000	50
1000–2000	75
2000–3000	275
3000–4000	100
	Total 500

D2 (a)

Weight in grams	Cumulative frequency
up to 20	23
up to 40	97
up to 60	223
up to 80	327
up to 100	389
up to 120	400

(b)

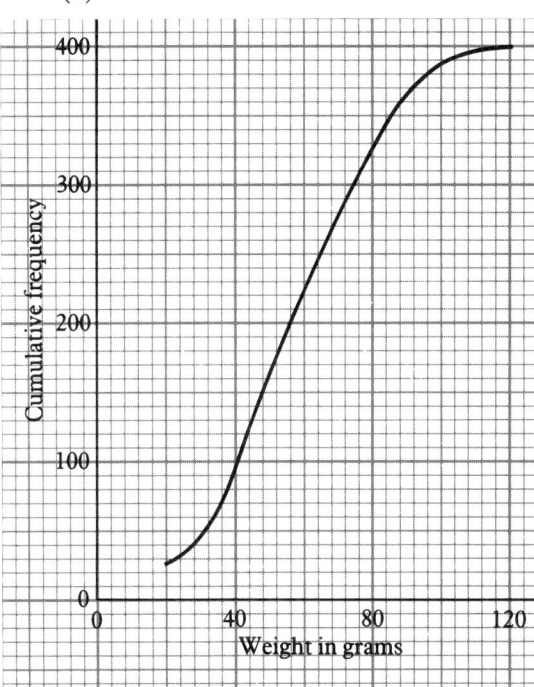

Median 56 g (approx.)

D3 (a)

Earnings in pounds	Cumulative number of employees
up to 50	38
up to 60	268
up to 80	289
up to 100	306
up to 150	309
up to 200	336
up to 250	350

(b) There is no point in drawing a smooth curve in this case.

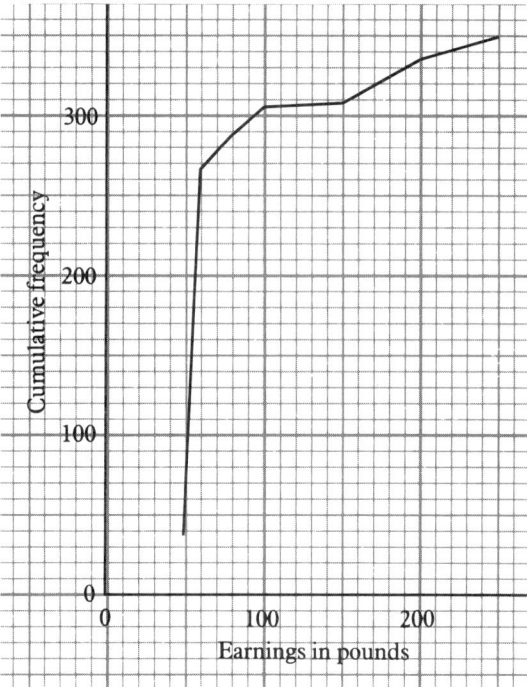

Median £55 (approx.)

D4 (a)

Earnings in pounds	Mid-interval value in pounds	Number of employees	Contribution to total, in pounds
0– 50	25	38	950
50– 60	55	230	12 650
60– 80	70	21	1 470
80–100	90	17	1 530
100–150	125	3	375
150–200	175	27	4 725
200–250	225	14	3 150
Totals		350	24 850

Estimated mean £71

(b) The median gives a better idea.
Discussion will be needed as to why this is so.

Review 3

14 Volume

14.1 84 cm³   **14.2** 177 cm   **14.3** (a) 7·70 cm³ (b) 68·5 g (both to 3 s.f.)

14.4 (a) $1000\,\text{m}^3$
(b) (i) $2000\,\text{m}^3$ (approx.)
(ii) $4000\,\text{m}^3$ (approx.)

14.5 (a) $0\cdot708\,\text{m}$ (b) $5\cdot67\,\text{m}^3$ (both to 3 s.f.)

14.6 (a) $168\,\text{cm}^3$ (b) $20\cdot9\,\text{cm}^3$
(c) $70\cdot7\,\text{cm}^3$ (all to 3 s.f.)

15 Problems in planning

15.1 (a) Here is one of the many possible solutions. Pupils could be asked to discuss whether some of the possible solutions are better than others.

Week no.	1	2	3	4	5	6
Clerk 1		■	■			■
Clerk 2		■				■
Clerk 3	■			■	■	
Clerk 4	■				■	

(b) If only two clerks are allowed away at any one time there is only a total of 10 weeks holiday available in a 5-week period.
But the total number of weeks holiday needed is 12, so it is impossible.

16 · Linear equations

16.1 (a) $a = 2$, $b = 5$ (b) $p = 6$, $q = 1$
(c) $s = 4$, $t = 4$

16.2 $(2\cdot5, 5\cdot75)$

16.3 (a) Let x be the cost in £ of a bottle of Gutrotwein von Deutschland and y be the cost in £ of a bottle of Suave Vino Bianco d'Italia
(b) $2x + 5y = 13\cdot70$
$4x + 3y = 14\cdot10$
(c) $x = 2\cdot1$, $y = 1\cdot9$
A bottle of Gutrotwein costs £2·10.
A bottle of Suave costs £1·90.

16.4 (a) $(4, {}^-3)$ (b) $(8, 3)$
(c) $(2\tfrac{2}{19}, {}^-\tfrac{11}{19})$ or $(2\cdot11, {}^-0\cdot58)$ (to 2 d.p.)

17 · Distributions

17.1 (a) 18000 (b) 2000 (c) 2:21 p.m.
(d) Lower quartile 2:06 p.m., upper quartile 2:28 p.m.

15.2

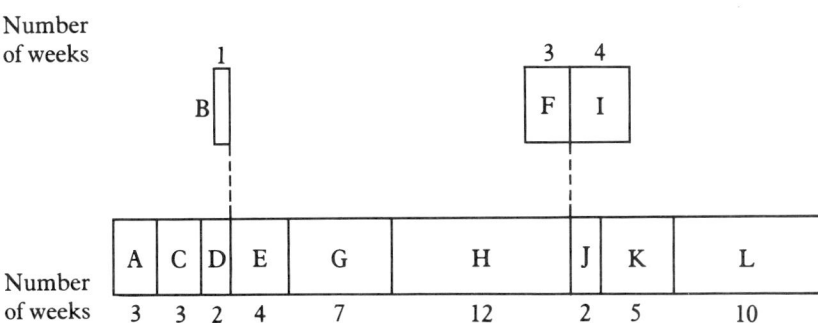

48 weeks

17.2 (a) A, 3·3 miles; B, 4·4 miles
(b)

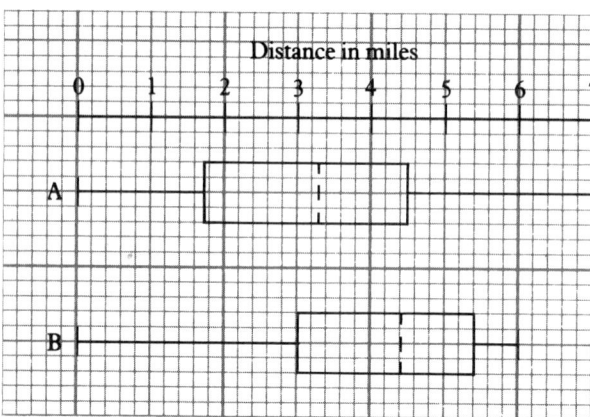

(c) In town B shoppers travel further on the whole.

17.3 (a)

Height in metres	Cumulative frequency
up to 15	19
up to 20	47
up to 25	81
up to 30	111
up to 35	124
up to 40	127

(b)

(c) About 22 m or 23 m

M   Miscellaneous

M1 (a) 72°   (b) 4·13 cm (to 3 s.f.)
(c) 61·9 cm^2
(d) (i) 247·7 cm^2 (ii) 557·4 cm^2 (both to 1 d.p.)

M2 (a) $x = 1·4$ (b) $x = 48·5$
(c) $x = 0·3$

M3 (a) Rotation of 90° anticlockwise, centre (0, ⁻2)
(b) Reflection in the line $y = {}^-x - 2$
(c) Reflection in the line $y = x$
(d) Reflection in the y-axis

M4 (a) $J_1 J_2$, $J_1 Q$, $J_1 K$, $J_1 A$
$J_2 Q$, $J_2 K$, $J_2 A$
$Q K$, $Q A$
$K A$

(b) $\frac{1}{10}$

M5 (a) np (b) $\frac{np + q}{n + 1}$

M6 If the cost of a sausage is s p,
the cost of an egg is e p,
the cost of bacon is b p,
and the cost of chips is c p,
then adding everything gives
$3(s + e + c + b) = 291$.
So $s + e + c + b = 97$.
Now subtracting each line in turn gives
$b = 27$, $s = 18$, $e = 13$, $c = 39$
So the cost of a sausage is 18p,
the cost of an egg is   13p,
the cost of bacon is   27p,
and the cost of chips is   39p.

M7 If the number of rabbits is r
and the number of hutches is h,
then $h + 1 = r$
and $\frac{r}{2} + 1 = h$.

Solving these equations simultaneously
gives $r = 4$, $h = 3$.
So there are 4 rabbits and 3 hutches.